Ancestral Inheritance:
The Yearly Cycle of Germanic Customs and Festivals

DER JAHRESRING

ANCESTRAL INHERITANCE

The Yearly Cycle of Germanic Customs and Festivals

JOSEPH OTTO PLASSMANN

Translated and Annotated by C.J. Miller

With Wood-carved Illustrations by Eugen Nerdinger

ANTELOPE HILL PUBLISHING

Dedicated to my wife for her patience, her assistance, and her encouragement, and to my Gothar for pushing me not-so-gently to take on this project.

– C.J. Miller

CONTENTS

TRANSLATOR FOREWORD

The author of this book, Joseph Otto Plassmann, was born to a middle-class family in 1895 in the small town of Warendorf in northwestern Germany, the son of a school-teacher and a housewife. He attended a Catholic school and then a *Gymnasium*, an academic school in the German-speaking world with a focus on preparing students for university. He later attended the University of Münster, studying Philology, the precursor to the more general field of Linguistics, focusing on written textual sources. He specialized in Germanic, English, and Romance Philology. During the First World War, he served in the infantry of the German Army, until he was severely wounded on the eastern front somewhere in Russia in 1914 or 1915. When he was sufficiently recovered, he held an administrative post in occupied Belgium, where he met Dutch folkish scholar Herman Wirth, a connection that would prove pivotal years later. After the war, he joined the *Einwohnerwehr* (Citizens' Defense), a right-wing nationalist paramilitary group that existed in violation of the Treaty of Versailles, which strictly limited the amount of armed forces Germany was allowed to maintain. In 1921 he received his doctorate for a dissertation on the writings of Hadewijch, a mysterious female Dutch poet and mystic of the thirteenth century. During this time, he also began writing nationalist and "folkish"-themed articles, and the focus of his studies increasingly went to this area.

In 1927 he became acquainted with Wilhelm Teudt, an eccentric amateur archaeologist whose outlandish theories proposed the idea that prior to the Roman invasions and later conversion to Christianity, there had been an advanced civilization in Northern Germany, which somehow had left only extremely fragmentary evidence behind, which Teudt intended to piece together to prove his theories. Plassmann considered Teudt amateurish and ill-informed, but they shared an interest in Germanic studies, and the two founded the Association of Friends of Ancient Germanic History and began publishing the journal *Germanien: Monthly Journal of Germanic Studies*, mainly including articles by Plassmann, Teudt, and Herman Wirth. In 1929, he joined the National Socialist War Victims' Association, the beginning of his official affiliation with the NSDAP.

In 1935, Herman Wirth, Heinrich Himmler, and agriculturalist Richard Walther Darré founded the *Forschungsgemeinschaft Deutsches Ahnenerbe* (Research Community for German Ancestral Heritage, often shortened to *Ahnenerbe*[1]), a branch of the SS dedicated to investigating the ancient origins and ways of life of the Germanic peoples. The organization was involved in archaeological excavations around Europe, as well as textual scholarship, and communicated its findings to other scholars and the public with various books, journals, conferences, and presentations. It also famously undertook a number of research expeditions to

---

[1] Pronounced "AHN-en-AIR-beh."

exotic locales such as Crimea, Iraq, and Tibet, searching for evidence of ancient "Aryan" civilization. Plassmann's journal *Germanien* was adopted by and absorbed into the *Ahnenerbe* later in 1935 under the influence of Herman Wirth, and Plassmann thus became a member, working full-time researching, writing for, and editing his journal.

Interest in research of this sort reached a peak during the National Socialist era, but it was by no means new. The Romantic movement of the late eighteenth to mid-nineteenth centuries coincided with the rise of modern nationalism in Europe. This Romantic nationalism brought about a new interest in the origins, histories, and cultures of peoples. Many artists across Europe in fields from painting to poetry began to look to their own national myths, and even pre-Christian mythologies, for inspiration, rather than biblical or classical Greek and Roman subject matter. In Germanic Northern Europe, this manifested in a renewed interest in writings originating from or depicting pagan times. Common folk and peasants were romanticized as the bearers of the most genuine and ancient ethnic customs and beliefs, untainted by education or exposure to other cultures. It was primarily on this basis that the brothers Jacob and Wilhelm Grimm interviewed ordinary people, especially but not exclusively peasants, to obtain and transcribe into writing their orally-transmitted stories, thus curating an "official record" of authentically German folktales and mythology. Their work created the most well-known literary versions of many fairy tales and stories now widely considered "classics," including Rapunzel, Snow White, Hansel and Gretel, and dozens more. Analogous undertakings occurred in Norway, Russia, France, and Italy.

Even as the era of literary and artistic romanticism subsided, the interest in folklore, mythology, and ethnic tradition continued. Pre-Christian, pagan themes and early poetic accounts of Germanic mythology inspired composer Wilhelm Richard Wagner's work, especially his operas. Romantic nationalism essentially morphed into what became known as the *völkisch* movement, a set of thinkers, organizations, and ideas promoting German ethnic nationalism and the notion that the German people must be restored to its ancient greatness.

The root word *Volk*, while obviously cognate with the English word *folk*, is used much more commonly and has slightly different connotations. The best translation in this context is perhaps *ethnicity*, denoting a people with a shared heritage, history, language, and culture; this leaves room for the more "racial" implications of the term that were bound up with the *völkisch* movement, as well as the more general use of *Volk* as simply "a people," for which it is still in common use in modern German today. *Völkisch* thus may be rendered as "folkish," but in the context of the movement, this must be understood as encompassing both the "racial" and cultural (or even "folksy") connotations of the term.

Mystical esoteric currents emerged within the *völkisch* movement, such as the neo-pagan "Ariosophy" ("Wisdom of the Aryans") of Austrian occultist and amateur runologist Guido von List, and the more Christian-influenced but undoubtedly heretical secret society *Ordo Novi Templii* (Order of the New Templars) of former Austrian monk Jörg Lanz von Liebenfells, founded in 1907 in an attempt to synthesize a Germanic ethnic religion from both Christian and pagan elements. The later *Germanenorden* (Germanic Order, sometimes translated Teutonic Order) founded in 1912 was more explicitly antisemitic and political in nature, otherwise continuing in the same tradition of the broader *völkisch* movement. In 1918, the more historically noteworthy Thule Society was founded in Munich as an offshoot of the soon-defunct *Germanenorden*. Its name derives ultimately from a lost account by ancient Greek explorer Pytheas of his alleged voyage to the furthest north point of the world. Later on, the Latin phrase *Ultima Thule* came to be used metaphorically for the far north, or generally for remote and unknown lands. Esoteric Aryanists of the late nineteenth and early twentieth centuries equated Thule with Hyperborea, a land in ancient Greek legend at the northern tip of the world, and sometimes even with the lost island of Atlantis, with some speculation that this land was the original homeland of the Aryans.

The *völkisch* movement persisted well into the twentieth century, strongly intersecting with all manner of right-wing nationalist thinkers and groups. Many of its ideas, key figures, and even organizations were eventually integrated into the burgeoning National Socialist movement. The Thule Society raised funds for the fledgling *Deutsche Arbeiterpartei*, the original name of the NSDAP, in 1919. It also originally founded the *Münchener Beobachter* newspaper, which eventually became the *Völkischer Beobachter* (*Folkish Observer*) and was purchased by the NSDAP in 1920. The Thule Society dissolved in 1925, but its ideas were carried forward by various far-right circles and esoteric scholars, and several Thule associates, including Gottfried Feder, Rudolf Heß, and Alfred Rosenberg, became prominent members of the NSDAP.

Coinciding with the era of Romantic nationalism was the early development of the field we now know as Indo-European Studies. During the Middle Ages, and even up to the eighteenth century, the prevailing view was that all languages must have originated from Hebrew. Beginning in the seventeenth century, various scholars began systematically drawing comparisons to prove relationships between European languages. European contact with India led some early pioneers, including Portuguese and Italian explorers, to notice similarities between Sanskrit and their own languages. In a 1767 letter sent from his post in India to a French scholarly society, French Jesuit and philologist Gaston-Laurent Couerdoux was the first to demonstrate linguistic affinity between Sanskrit, Latin, and Greek. In 1786, William Jones, an English philologist assigned to a colonial legal post in India, who was unaware of Couerdoux's previous speculation, proposed a proto-language ancestral to the Sanskrit, Persian, Greek, Latin, Germanic, and Celtic languages, which he termed the Indo-Aryan language group. Although he incorrectly suggested ancient Egyptian, Chinese, and Japanese may be related as well, and he overlooked the Slavic languages, the core of his theory has proven sound, and is considered a breakthrough in linguistics, foundational to the modern field of comparative linguistics, and the first systematic evidence for the existence of the now undisputed Indo-European language family.

Building on Jones' theory, scholars throughout the nineteenth and early twentieth centuries began compiling evidence in the fields of comparative religion and mythology, history, archaeology, and especially linguistics, of the ancient roots common to all Indo-European languages and peoples. In these early stages, the word Aryan was much more broadly applied than it is today, and quite without any stigma or prejudice attached to it. The term is etymologically linked to the ancient Greek ἀρετή (*Arete*—excellence, virtue, moral good) and aristocracy ("rule by the best"). Among other terms, Aryan was commonly used as shorthand for the Indo-European languages and peoples, although it had only ever been self-applied as an ethnic term by the Indo-Aryan peoples of Iran, Central Asia, and India.

During the late nineteenth century and into the National Socialist era, *völkisch* scholars conflated the concept of Aryan with Germanic exceptionalism, as well as Nordicist racial theory, which held that the stereotypically Nordic pheno-type—tall, fair-skinned, blond-haired, blue-eyed, et cetera—was the prevailing phenotype among the original ancient Aryans, and thus evidence of the purest Aryan heritage. Going further still, Nordicist esoteric-Aryanists such as Alfred Rosenberg, Heinrich Himmler, and, it seems, the author of this book, Joseph Otto Plassmann, rejected any foreign influence, including Christianity, which they viewed as Semitic and alien, in their desire to reconstruct a purely Aryan worldview. The Northern European hypothesis, a holdover of the nineteenth century, retained its currency in the National Socialist era, postulating Northern Europe as the original homeland of the ancient Aryans.

All of this historical baggage, especially the association with National Socialism and Nordicism, has made the use of the word Aryan a taboo when used in reference to a people. Today, outside of being employed to ridicule belief in a European race, the term is basically relegated to the field of linguistics, in reference to the Indo-Aryan language sub-family, the descendants of Vedic Sanskrit. Modern main-stream scholarship universally rejects the Northern European hypothesis, placing the earliest verifiable homeland of the proto-Indo-Europeans somewhere on the Pontic-Caspian Steppe in what is now southern Russia, southeastern Ukraine, and western Kazakhstan. Cutting-edge genetic research indicates that while "Nordic"-type features were certainly more common among some Indo-European peoples than other groups, blond hair, blue eyes, and fair skin were likely not the predominant phenotype among the proto-Indo-Europeans.

And yet, despite these corrections, despite the taboo, the deconstruction, and the attempts to prove otherwise, modern archaeological, linguistic, and in recent years especially genetic research has essentially vindicated the core truths of those earlier Aryan studies. It can no longer be credibly denied that all of the various Indo-European peoples share a certain element of linguistic, cultural, historical, and to some extent even genetic heritage. Though a modern scholar in the field of Indo-European studies might scoff at the idea that he or she is engaged in the spiritual successor to the Aryan studies of the nineteenth and early twentieth centuries, the fact is that the subject matter has remained essentially the same; only some of the terminology, methods, and underlying assumptions have changed.

Scholarly and public interest in the early forebears of European civilization has continued unabated, especially interest in ancient European religion, mythology, and culture. For evidence of this interest, look no further than the recent cultural fascination with all things "Viking," especially among Europeans and those descended from them. This fascination is easily accounted for: the Germanic peoples of the Viking era were the last to convert to Christianity, remaining pagan the longest; thus, compared to earlier converts, most is known about their way of life, spiritual beliefs, and stories. Perhaps in this recent Viking fascination in popular culture there is also an element of pride—even if subconscious for many—in the image of European people, not so different from ourselves, who were not yet domesticated, who were wild, and widely feared. In an age whose prevailing cultural norms encourage domestication, a degree of romanticizing the noble savage of the European past is understandable.

This book certainly contains an element of that, albeit less focused on the Vikings of Scandinavia and more on the continental Germans. First published in 1941, *Ancestral Inheritance* is Plassmann's exploration, and indeed exaltation, of the inherited customs and beliefs of, first and foremost, the ethnic Germans, the Germanic peoples more broadly, and occasional insights on themes that reach back even further into the common Indo-European past. Some of the claims may be outdated or dubious in light of modern scholarship, and these are generally noted as such in the footnotes of the text, but there is also insightful and original thought and a broad presentation of the scholarship on the subject at the time. Plassmann explores the underlying meaning and symbolism of festivals and myths associated with various times of the year chronologically, beginning and ending with the winter solstice, such that the structure of the book parallels the cycle of the year, with each chapter devoted to a particular festival, cultural motif, folktale, or myth, and often all of the above.

Much of what in this book, and in the scholarship of Plassmann's time and place, was assumed to be particular to Germanic spirituality, in fact applies to ancient Indo-European spirituality generally, and this becomes truer especially as one zooms out from specific details to observe the general principles. That is to say: while names, dates, and details differ, for example between the Germanic and the Celtic tradition, the broader underlying ideas, themes, and values are held in common by all Indo-European cultures, as they all share a common heritage. And therein lies the enduring significance of this book: it represents an early exploration of pre-Christian, Indo-European spirituality and tradition, with a Germano-centric focus, but whose deeper insights and truths apply to all peoples and cultures descended from Indo-European origins.

– C.J. Miller

INTRODUCTION

Through our time runs a sense of remembrance of a distant and seemingly long-gone world of experience: a world that once signified security and comfort for our ancestors, in all their conflicts and struggles, and gave them the secure feeling of being enveloped and protected in a greater order within the narrow circle of their existence. Arching over this world was the bright hall that was built above the broad earth by the constant orbit of the sun itself, which was renewed year after year: it was the high hall of the sun, which the Eddas call the hall of *Gimlé*,[2] the stronghold of all order. By this structure, the master builder of the world himself let us recognize the laws, according to which all life, becoming and passing away, takes place. The life of the individual, however, was not, as it may seem to us today, a path that appears from somewhere out of the dark void, only to lose itself again in

---

[2] A place associated with the afterlife in Germanic mythology, mentioned in the Eddic poem *Völuspá*.

the void; rather, it was a thread that could not be separated from the great fabric upon which the circling celestial bodies incessantly weave. And when it seemingly disappeared from the bright house of summer existence—to plunge into the wintry darkness below the edge of the visible world—this was nothing compared to the certainty that the path of life, like the path of the sun, would again lead with the same necessity back up over the edge of the dark world.

In this recognition, the sanctity of life dawned on the ancient generations, and on it rests our entire morality even today, if only we are able to see its roots, insofar as it is more than the observance of a dead precept. It is a morality that no zealous preacher will ever be able to give us, but that still pervades us today, uplifting us portentously when we stand in the towering hall of a German cathedral, which is indeed none other than a reflection of that high, light-flooded hall of the sun of which the old poets spoke. But this recognition is also the source of that heroic spirit that is as joyful as the sun, because even the battlefield of hard life is subject to its laws, for it is itself the archetype and model of the hero, who joyfully treads his path to victory. For our ancestors, however, only a few hundred years ago, the word "pious" also had the meaning "courageous," and so their piety was the fulfillment of a courageous mood of the soul that cherished the spark of heroism as a precious treasure.

The old faith seemed to have long since been broken, eradicated, and replaced by a new doctrine. All the piety and holiness of our Germanic life, as well as the words stolen from us, seemed to have been taken into a foreign administration that tried to offer us the bread from our own father's house, mixed with foreign ingredients, and made almost unrecognizable and inedible, as a gift from a foreign land. But this foreign power has not penetrated into the deepest parts of our soul. The old world order with its piety, displaced from conscious life, withdrew into the poetic and the unconscious, which in myth and fairy tale allowed deeper landscapes of the soul to blossom than any doctrine preached to the ears could ever do. It also remained alive in the customs of the people, which from time immemorial have given wonderful shape to their faith and their unity. Thus, the old faith still lives today as a spark under the ashes. If one regards it correctly, that which has been erected against it and above it has itself only retained its vitality insofar as it was able to draw from the suppressed and repressed Germanic spiritual heritage.

Today, however, we face the danger that this spiritual heritage, impoverished and dispossessed, will be completely lost to us. A thousand years of being superimposed with foreign ways of thinking have made us question with our intellect that which was once unquestionable and self-evident to the knowing mind. The intentional has more and more taken the place of the emergent, but perhaps that is precisely why our longing has become all the stronger. We long to find our way back to the half-buried sources and to regain from them the sanctity of life that gave our ancestors their inner security in bravery and loyalty. Today, however, this is only possible by way of full consciousness, if we reverently engage with the ancient sacred ideas and try to represent their content in our language.

The following representations have arisen from this intention over the course of several years. They are written from the experience of the course of the year and are informally placed here again in the cycle of the Germanic year, as our ancestors experienced it. They have emerged from the experience of what lives in us as memory, and what science has recognized and proven. But they are not scientific essays in the usual sense; they aim to bring back to life and transfuse into living material what still lives as an echo, and what a science serving the national revival has collected from earlier times, insofar as it concerns real life-values. Admittedly, these are only a few pieces from the treasury of the eternal Germanic spirit, and yet they speak to us like something long familiar. The real old gold, we hope, will still shine in them, and restore to many people something of the old ancestral heritage. May the individual reader find his way back in silence with this book to that old and eternally young land of our native faith; may larger circles seek together the path to the sources of our being; we hope that the purpose of this book will be fulfilled for all: to be a guide to the eternal values of the Germanic soul.

1

Winterwende–Jahreswende

THE TURN OF WINTER—THE TURN OF THE YEAR

All life is struggle and victory. Victory, however, is the commitment to ever new struggles. Therefore, struggle itself is the highest content of the victorious life.

This is the heroic confession of the Teuton translated into our language. It is a confession that expresses the experience and the echo of the eternal struggle that the ancestors of the Germans once had to fight in primordial times against the eternal ice of the north. In this struggle lie the roots of our strength, our spirit, our faith, and our ethos.

In the barren north, where the fire of the sun only offered the northern man sparse opportunity for life in a tenacious struggle with the ice, the world view of the Teuton arose. His life was a struggle with darkness and cold, and other than his own strength and ability, he had no other ally in this struggle but the sun, which year after year for a few short months rose out of the mist and darkness and gave him a short but wonderfully bright summer. Thus, the sun became for the Teuton the archetype and the symbol of his own power, the symbol of the divine spark, which he felt as a constant obligation to the heroic life. The life of the sun in its short annual cycle, in its joyful, bright summer day, and in its dark wintry absorption became for him a symbol of his own life, which set for him a high task: the obligation to fight the darkness and all the evil powers that threaten the pure spark of life.

From the north, the northern spirit and northern blood radiated in ever new waves over the inhabited earth, and everywhere it brought with it its high worldview, which was a worldview of light, a heroic worldview of constant, restless struggle. But the struggle of light is not a matter for unhappy, sullen souls. It bears its reward, its joyfulness, for joy was and is the keynote of all true heroism.

Joy animated the battle-hardened northern hosts who created states and high intellectual cultures in faraway India and in the mountains of Iran. Joyful heroism lived in the unforgettable deeds of the ancient Greeks, who are closely related to us. And the Germanic hosts were joyful and heroic, who, in the storms of the migration period, shattered the old and the rotten and created a new, Germanic Europe in its place. Wherever a poet or thinker of northern blood and spirit gave form to his highest creed, he drew it from the ancient parable of his primordial ancestors' experience, which still lived and shone in our great poet:

> Joyously, as his suns speed
> Through Heaven's glorious order,
> Hasten, Brothers, on your way,
> Exulting as a knight in victory.[3]

The sun is the creator of all living things for the northern man. With the fire of the sun, the northern Prometheus brought

---

[3] From Ludwig van Beethoven's "Ode to Joy."

the divine light from heaven to earth and ignited the fire that will never be extinguished as long as the great light of heaven is above us, and as long as heroic hearts beat here on earth, shaping the legacy of the ancestors into new life from purity of blood and spirit. No people, however, has preserved this ancient and sacred legacy so faithfully, despite all hostility and attempts to falsify it, as the German people, who in their hard struggle with the land, with winter night, and the power of ice, have kept the heroic meaning and the old symbols alive in the depths of their minds.

The German gives deep and essential expression to his heroic worldview in his annual festivals. They celebrate the battle of light against cold and darkness. In the old, sacred festival of the winter solstice, the German celebrates the rebirth of light from the night of the year; in the high fires of Easter, he celebrates the triumphant resurrection of the light of heaven to the great heroic deeds of spring and summer. He celebrates the triumph of light at the height of summer, when the sun reaches the highest point in its annual course. Then the fires from the heights greet the sun again, the great parable of one's own life in its becoming and passing, for the heroic northerner knows that in all becoming there is a decay. Just as the sun descends from its triumphant heights into the darkness of the winter night, so he himself will descend from the height of life into the darkness of death. But the spark of divine life never goes out: like the sun, it will rise again and take up the battle with darkness anew.

Life is struggle, and every living community is a community of struggle. At the turn of the year, when the experience of struggle is symbolized particularly vividly, the community must also experience its most powerful immersion. The sun fires with which we celebrate the holy night of the year are the most profound celebrations of our ethnic community, especially that fire that, along with the victory of the reborn sun, also celebrates the fruit of the year's communal work, when barn and storehouse are full of the year's golden fruit, when there are mysterious whispers in the air about the hunt of the god who carries everything dead away with him in a storm to return it to new life in the roar of the universe.[4]

Thus, the wintergreen tree, the tree of the year and the tree of life, rises from one year to the next and shines as the "radiant banner of God," as our ancestors called it, before the rows of the coming years and generations. In former times, burning discs whirled through the air all over Germania, and torchbearers walked and still walk here and there around the snowy fields, binding the nascent power of the sun to the power of mother earth. And to the dead who belonged to the community of struggle, the living consecrated their toasts.

All this, which has been faithfully preserved in the depths of the German spirit as the indestructible core of our being, we wish to bring back to life and make visible. When the fires of the sun blaze up, we know their old and eternally new meaning: "Preserve the holy spark in which God revealed himself to the ancestors and to you in the northern winter night!"

---

[4] Possibly a reference to the Wild Hunt (or Wild Host), a folklore motif found in Northern Europe with various regional names about a rowdy band of hunters or warriors on horseback raging through the night sky accompanied by dogs and wolves, usually led by the god Odin (*Woden* or *Wotan*), but occasionally by a nobleman cursed to hunt eternally, or even sometimes by a female figure known as Holda, Frau Holle, or Berta. The reference here is not entirely clear, and the symbolic context that Plassmann attributes to it here is not consistent with traditional interpretations of the Wild Hunt.

2

Vom Sinn der Fasnacht

ON THE MEANING OF FASNACHT (KARNEVAL)

Many things that today seem to have become empty and
meaningless habits of rootless city dwellers still have their
roots in the soil of thousands of years of tradition, on which
the deepest experience once grew, which reaches from
ancient times into our own day. The symbols of these
customs still include the symbols of the world order as our
ancestors recognized them, but also the tools and devices
with which they once fought the great battle for light and life.
They not only fought this battle with dogged skill and
endurance, but they also knew how to celebrate victory in the
eternal struggle to secure and preserve life. Even the hard-
working and serious northerner could become high-spirited,
exuberantly filled with the breath of life, during these victory
celebrations. With his close connection to life and the course
of the all-sustaining sun, the northerner experiences this
exuberance especially when the life-giver emerges
triumphantly from the confinement of winter and, as a
liberated queen, radiantly begins her course to the heights of
summer.

9

No wonder that the man of the north, who was truly a man of freedom ever since he was first lured out of his winter home by the invigorating power of the heavenly light, went "out of his mind" in the truest sense of the word. The irrepressible air of carefully-nurtured life took over him anew, and the youth of the year tempted him to high-spirited action. This unrestrained exuberance, which turns things upside down and overcomes all that is stiff, old, and all-too-dignified through cheerful ridicule, is the other aspect of the Germanic man, who, between ice and sun, the serious and the cheerful, grasps the full meaning of life.

Herein lies the deeper meaning of our *Fasnacht* or *karneval* customs, which originally have nothing to do with the Church's fasting commandment, nor did they get their name from it. The name rather refers to the celebration nights of the growing and fruit-ripening life. This meaning is still recognized above all where the customs have been preserved more genuinely and meaningfully in rural seclusion than in the soul-sucking big city. There, too, raucous merriment is the keynote of the celebrations, but the joy is even more innate and genuine because it is closer to its deeper origins. In many cases, people still walk through the fields with burning torches, "to wake up the grain," as they say, and to tell it symbolically of the triumph and ascent of life. There are certain things again that only the children, the most constant preservers of ancient customs, have preserved in their games and songs. In their spring games they still recall the maiden with the golden hair, who was locked up by the evil giant in the dark tower or in the maze and who is now freed by the youthful hero and led to the bridal procession. Even on the asphalt of the big city, they still play the age-old game of heaven and hell, or of the snail's shell, the image of the winter sun's orbit, which as the "Troy Town" in some places still forms the age-old scene of the game of the liberation of the maiden.[5]

In many cases, these games are far apart in the calendar, for the Church drove a wedge into the middle of the joyous festive season by introducing Lent. And so one finds the same customs again partly in the spring, partly in the summer. And it was precisely the call to strict penance that increased the festive air in the last days before Lent to that wild frenzy that we find today at *karneval* time, especially in those cities where Lent is still observed. What is the meaning of the word *karneval*, under which this old spring festival is celebrated not only in Germany, but also in southern Europe? The word is Latin, the custom originally Germanic.[6] *Carrus Navalis* is a

---

[5] "Troy Town" refers to turf or stone labyrinths on hillsides or hilltops found primarily in Britain, Scandinavia, and the Baltic coasts. The name refers to the walls of the ancient city of Troy, which were said to be labyrinthine. Most were constructed during the medieval period, though earlier examples of the motif from southern Europe are found on coins and rock carvings dating as far back as the seventh century BC. The symbolic significance of these labyrinths is debated. Whether they have any connection at all to Troy is uncertain; those found on the isle of Crete are instead connected with the labyrinth in the Greek myth of Theseus and the Minotaur. Some of the more recent examples around the Baltic coast are associated with seafarers, who would walk to the center of the maze, enticing evil spirits to follow them and get lost in the maze, then run out to their ships and put out to sea before the evil spirits could follow. In Sweden they are associated with fertility rites where a boy must navigate the maze without touching the stones to reach a fair maiden at the center. An Etruscan example, one of the oldest, is a rock carving that depicts two couples making love next to the maze, again indicating a connection to fertility. A singular explanation for the symbolic significance of the motif is probably impossible, as it has been used over a wide geographical area throughout many centuries, and thus its names, interpretations, and the traditions surrounding it have evolved with time and place. Plassmann's interpretation, while perhaps unorthodox, can thus neither be confirmed nor disproven by current scholarship.

[6] A dubious claim.

ship set on wheels, [7] which in ancient times was sailed through the countryside as a symbol of the coming of spring, filled with joyful, noisy people, bringing tidings to states and people of the triumph of new life. This is an old custom of seafaring peoples, for whom the resumption of navigation was the most important event of the new year. We know that in Germanic times the divine figure of Nehalennia, [8] as the liberated virgin was called at that time, sailed through the lands of the Lower Rhine. In legends and fairy tales, the savior with the sheaf comes floating from unknown lands on this ship; it brings the Lohengrin[9] of our legend with the spring bird, the holy swan; it also carries the holy tree of the year, at whose roots it lay in the July night. The ship's chariot with the merry fools has served as a festive symbol throughout the Middle Ages; the poet Sebastian Brant tried to castigate the countless fools of all mankind under its image.[10]

---

[7] *Carrus Navalis*: literally "naval wagon" in Latin, a ship (or a parade float) that takes part in Carnival parade processions, mostly in parts of Latin Europe, as well as in Mardi Gras festivities in New Orleans. It has been suggested that the word Carnival is etymologically derived from the term CARrus NAVALis. The tradition may date all the way back to ancient Roman times and the *Navigium Isis* (vessel of Isis), a procession by the mystery religion cult of the goddess Isis.
[8] A Germanic or possibly Celtic goddess found in depictions mostly around the North Sea coast of continental Europe, especially around what is now the Netherlands, associated with seafaring. She is often depicted with a basket of apples, loaves of bread, or ship parts, with a faithful dog looking up at her, sometimes near a ship.
[9] A character unique to German adaptations of Arthurian legend. He appears on a boat pulled by swans. The most famous adaptation is Richard Wagner's 1848 opera of the same name.
[10] Fifth-century German humanist, legal scholar, and poet, best known for his book *Daß Narrenschyff* (*The Ship of Fools*), a satire of social issues of the day, including public conduct and controversies in the Catholic Church. The book draws on the motif of the ship of fools that originated in Plato's *Republic*, depicting a ship sailed by an incompetent captain and crew. Plato's original allegory was

What the ship is to seafaring peoples, the plough is to farmers, and even today we find it among the life-awakening springtime. In Saxony, on Candlemas Day,[11] when work by artificial light ceases according to the old labor codes, the plough is harnessed by jesters and driven through lanes and fields with the cheerful crack of whips and all kinds of merry nonsense, to awaken the people and the fields and to announce the resumption of tillage. We also find this plough on the prehistoric rock paintings of the north, which are at least equal in age and significance to their much more famous Egyptian counterparts.

Even the *karneval* prince, who today is celebrated like a king, and even his wife, have a genealogy that goes far back into Germanic prehistory. We have very old reports of a huge doll, in which a human being was often hidden, being paraded around festively, as is still the custom in southern countries today. In Flanders, they call him the giant and celebrate him like a king returning to his kingdom after a long absence and who—as it used to be—has freed the maiden from the imprisonment of the winter giant in a foreign country, in order to lead her home in a festive procession. We see that it is spring itself that is heralded by this symbol; the festive bridal procession that his own procession actually represents is the ancient myth of the marriage of heaven and earth, which takes place in the awakening of the motherly earth by the rays of the youthful sun. The parading of this "giant" is depicted on a Germanic rock carving that is several thousand years old, and thus probably the oldest representation of a carnival procession.

Cheerfulness and the breath of life and overflowing joy of

---

intended to make the point that governance must be based on expert knowledge rather than mob rule.
[11] February 2nd

being—not in flippant thoughtlessness, but as a deep, meaningful affirmation of life itself—that is the meaning of the merry *karneval*, which, as a complement to more serious celebrations, is also part of the heritage of our ancestors.

3

Vom Schwerttanz und den Schwertfechtern

ON THE SWORD-DANCE AND SWORD FIGHTERS

Seventy years ago, at *karneval* time in a small village in Westphalia, a strange procession could be seen: eight men carrying huge swords on their shoulders, led by a ninth, went from farm to farm. Wherever they went, the wide door of the hall was willingly opened for them; they walked around in a round dance for a short time and then, at the command of the ninth, the leader of the dance, crossed their swords together so that the sharp blades formed a large star. Each held his own sword in his right hand and the tip of his opponent's sword in his left, which was protected with straw to prevent injury. They would then begin to swing this sword-star up and down, and when they had built up some momentum, the lead dancer would boldly leap onto the center of the "rose." He would be flung up with it, fall back, and be flung up still higher the next time, to reach his swaying dance floor again each time with uncanny certainty. The game went on until the daring dancer reached the top of the roof with a swing, to which he clung, usually to catch a piece of booty, a ham, or a sausage. This was put into a large sack, and the swordsmen

15

moved on to collect more booty from other farmsteads with their daring game, which was then eaten at the communal feast.

And yet, of course, such life-threatening games were not played for the sake of this reward. To the Germanic, all play is a reflection of life, about whose hardness and dangerous nature he was never mistaken, but which he rather affirmed so completely that his games are for the most part fighting games. And when this iron-hard brotherhood, whose members all dared the dangerous dance in turn, ate the gifts they had won at the feast, they were probably expressing the idea that it is only fitting for a man to enjoy what he has won himself at the risk of life and limb. Thus, "playing" in the old German language also means "fencing," and just as the game is a reflection of life, he also understands life as a single game of combat that uplifts male courage. Almost two thousand years ago, the Roman author Tacitus already knew enough to report on this fighting game of the Germanic tribes:

> There is only one kind of spectacle among them, which recurs at every gathering. Naked young men, who play this game as a sport, perform a dangerous dance between swords and spears. It required skill, and this required grace. But they do not do it for gain or profit: the pleasure of the spectators is the only reward for such bold daring.[12]

Thus, the Roman probably did not fully grasp the meaning of the Germanic game. The lust for danger is what elevates the bold player and makes him fearsome and invincible in the great sword dance of battle; after all, up to the time of

---

[12] From *Germania*, an ethnographical account of the Germanic tribes written around AD 98 by Roman historian Publius Cornelius Tacitus.

mercenary armies, the tumult of battle was called a dance. And there is another meaning at play in this game: the battle between light and darkness is fought out in it—symbolically, yes, but no less dangerously. For this reason, we find the sword dance at the celebration of spring, which is the actual meaning of *Fasnacht*, and at wedding celebrations, which must be preceded by a test in the sword dance, which historically, and occasionally even in the present day, the bridegroom had to undergo. In the Middle Ages, Neidhart von Reuenthal[13] tells us in a song about such a spring play, which is called the "Easter play": in spring, the peasants tie on their shining long swords; Frideholt, the lead dancer, carries the sword, which elsewhere is called the "Easter salmon," and leads the crowd to the lawn, which lies in front of the *Dinghof* gate. The poet calls out to him that he should be brave and stand his ground in fencing, so that "Frau Künze" will be pleased, likely alluding to the fair lady of this peasant knight. But it is among the peasants that the ancient game has survived longest in its original form, and it has held on most tenaciously where the old peasant freedom has survived the longest. In a village in Lippe, up until sixty years ago, no one could marry into the peasantry unless he possessed a fencing sword, which was called a *pauk* there. In other words, the Germanic village association did not accept any man who did not prove himself capable of fighting and playing fighting games.

Thus, German folk tradition has also made its highest hero, King Dietrich von Bern,[14] into a sword dancer who performs

---

[13] A thirteenth-century German poet who wrote mostly in the *Minnesang* tradition, a medieval genre of songs about chivalry and courtly love.

[14] A mythologized version of real-life, fifth-century Gothic king and quasi-Roman Emperor Theodoric the Great. Theodoric is the

in a *karneval*-esque sword play. King Etzel is the lead dancer,[15] Dietrich's famous twelve companions are sword dancers, and it is he himself who finally slays the demonic challenger in a sword fight and frees the imprisoned maiden, reminiscent of the battle between summer and winter for the liberation of the sun maiden. Similarly, the heroic poem *Rosengarten zu Worms*[16] has become a sword-play in which Dietrich's heroes fight Kriemhild's men; the lead dancer and victor on Dietrich's side is old Hildebrand, whose name is also mentioned elsewhere in the sword-play. This reminds us that the underlying tone of all these sword-dance plays was, after all, a profoundly tragic one, for our oldest heroic saga tells of the fateful sword fight between father and son, in which Hildebrand slays his son Hadubrand.[17]

---

pseudo-latinized version of the Gothic name *Þiudareik*, equivalent to *Þiðrek* in Old Norse, or *Dietrich* in modern German.

[15] A similarly mythologized version of Attila the Hun. The allusions to Dietrich and Etzel are references to medieval Germanic heroic legends, semi-historical mythologized accounts of the great deeds of heroes, spread by oral tradition and later written down, mostly originating from the Migration Period of the fourth to sixth centuries AD, during which Germanic tribes spread across Europe and beyond.

[16] The name of a thirteenth-century poem about Dietrich von Bern; the translation of the title is *The Rose Garden at Worms*. Worms is a city in southwestern Germany.

[17] Referring to the ninth-century *Hildebrandslied* (*Song of Hildebrand*), the oldest known poetic text in Old High German, the earliest distinct stage of the language that branched off from the other Germanic languages to become modern German. It tells the story of a father and son, separated by fate at a young age, who meet each other on a battlefield as champions of opposing armies. The poem was first written down around AD 830, but is based on a much older oral tradition, one that has parallels in all Indo-European mythological traditions—for example, Cú Chulainn killing his son Conlaí in Irish mythology, and Ilya Muromets killing his son Podsokolnik in the Slavic version.

This tragic outcome is also depicted in our sword dances: a fencer sinks to the ground, seemingly dealt a fatal blow, and is carried out by the others on their swords. After some time, of course, he is awakened again, which again probably stems from the ancient myth of the death and rebirth of the hero. The fact that this play, which is highly tragic at its core, takes place at *karneval* time, at a time of the greatest revelry, only *appears* to be a contradiction. Of course, there is no sense of repentance behind it for the Germanic, but rather his knowledge of the two aspects of life: that of hard necessity, and that of cheerful confidence that comes from belief in the immortality of life. Thus, as in the old heroic songs, the Germanic knows how to joke about his own wounds and to dance between swords and spearheads.

4

Osterfeuer und Osterwasser

EASTER FIRE AND EASTER WATER

Streams and brooks are freed from the ice. The great wheel of the year and of life begins its upward course anew; the time of the first awakening of the irrepressible joy of new life gives way to a quieter and more contemplative, deeper and more introspective mood. The first rays of daylight shine brighter and earlier from the east: day catches up with night, and soon it outstrips its nocturnal brother in length. A time comes when the rise and fall of the great celestial light establishes the balance of day and night, as it appears in the east and disappears in the west, thus forming the great equilibrium in the year's cycle, from which the inexorable ascent to the summery heights then takes place.

The old, sacred meaning lives on today in the name and custom of this time of triumphant light. As the time of the lengthening days, our old German ancestors called it "Langizo," known to us as the fair *Lenz*, and is still called the

"Langes" in Tyrol today.[18] For more than a thousand years, our poets have sung of him as a youth with flowery hair—not unlike the youthful god Freyr,[19] who was celebrated by the farming ancestors of our prehistoric times as the bringer of Lenz and life, and whose golden-bristled boar made the last snow disappear on hills and slopes. But we know this great time of growth by the name "Easter time." We are hardly aware of what the name actually means, but its magic has remained unchanged through all the ages of alienation, adulteration, and suppression that have come upon our people over the millennia. Today, as in the past, the content of its experience means light and life and the dawning of a new age, and indeed this is also in its literal sense, which originally meant "new light." It is connected with the east, for when the light of heaven appears again exactly at the eastern point of the horizon, then the time of summer ascent has come: the upper half of the year has begun.

This new light was greeted from time immemorial with earthly fires that blazed from mighty wood piles on the mountains to announce victory and homecoming. Here, too, the message is passed from mountain to mountain, from peak

---

[18] *Langizo* is the reconstructed Proto-Germanic word for *long*. The words *langizo* (long) and *tinaz* (day) combined to give *langatinaz* (long-day), the Proto-Germanic word for the spring season. *Lenz* was the word for spring in Old High German, and is still used as a personification of the spring in certain expressions in modern German. *Langes* is the equivalent in the local dialect of South Tyrol, an ethnic German region of northern Italy. The point Plassmann is illustrating is that the linguistic origin of these words for spring is in the lengthening of the day.

[19] Freyr, sometimes called Ingwi-Frey or just Frey, is a Germanic god associated with peace, fertility, and kingship. His animal companion, which he either rides or is pulled by on a chariot, is a fearsome boar with glowing golden bristles. In Old Norse, the boar's name is *Gullinbursti* (Golden Bristles).

to peak, just as our ancestors proclaimed a great victory to the furthest of their people through these chains of fire. And the old custom went and still goes further, revealing a meaningful interpretation of life in its symbols: the wheel of the holy year itself is seized by the flames of new light and rolls over the earth, spraying light and fire. In many a quiet landscape, where the steamroller has not yet crushed everything, these wheels of fire still roll today, passed down from generation to generation with the sacred fire of blood and life itself, of which they are symbols. Many weeks beforehand, the straw is gathered and prepared with which the enormous wooden wheels are stuffed. This common preparation forms a joyful and tight-knit community, for it touches the inner core of the essence of all national community: the common orientation towards the eternal goal that is given to us all through blood and race. On the day of the festival, the wheels are rolled up the mountain, lit in the dark of night and set in motion down the valley. A whirlwind of flames rolls down, leaving a luminous trail behind them; in ever more powerful leaps the wheels race down to the valley—leaving the imprint of light on the fields with traces of fire until they burn out or are suddenly extinguished in the next stream or river. This used to happen in all Germanic regions; today, only in Hesse and Westphalia[20] has the custom been preserved in its old vitality.[21]

Various runic signs also herald the meaning of this triumphant time. The *mannaz* rune, which symbolizes the

---

[20] Hesse and Westphalia are two provinces in northwestern Germany.

[21] This passage refers to a spring tradition of lighting wagon wheels wrapped with straw and rolling them down a hill at night. The tradition continues today in some rural parts of Germany, France, and Switzerland. A similar tradition existed in Baltic and Slavic regions but was performed at Midsummer.

rise of light, is still preserved today as a sign of the Easter season in our traditional symbols.[22] In Friesland, Holland, and Westphalia, they are called "palm bushes"; they are three-forked sticks richly decorated with eggs, with various foliage, with the season's last apples, and with colorful ribbons. They are mirrored on a larger scale in the "Easter maypoles" that are erected here and there as a sign of spring; they are wrapped in straw and burnt to the ground. "The delight of man" is the name of the rune in the old rune poem,[23] and that

---

[22] The "*Mannaz*" rune ᛗ of the Elder Futhark and Anglo-Saxon Futhorc alphabets phonetically represents the /m/-phoneme, as occurs, for example, at the beginning of the word *man*. The symbolic association that Plassmann attributes to *Mannaz*, as well as the next sentence associating it with a three-forked shape, indicate that he is referring to the "*Mannaz*" of the pseudo-runic "Armanen Futharkh" alphabet invented by Austrian mystic and esoteric-nordicist Guido von List in 1902. Von List's "Armanen Futharkh" was itself essentially a bastardized version of the Younger Futhark alphabet, which replaced the Elder Futhark around the eighth century AD in Scandinavia, but was not used in Germany. In the Elder Futhark (and the "Armanen runes" that were derived from it) the /m/-phoneme was represented with the rune ᛦ, called the *Maðr* rune, whereas in the Elder Futhark and Anglo-Saxon Futhorc, this rune was known as *Algiz* and represented the /z/ or /ks/-phonemes. The phonetic values of the runes are known to scholars, as they were primarily an alphabet used for writing, but any symbolic significance of individual runes is a matter of interpretation and open to debate, thus any claims about what a particular rune supposedly "represents" aside from its phonetic value should be regarded with a degree of skepticism.

[23] The rune poems are a series of poems that list the letters of the runic alphabets with a poetic stanza relating to each rune in the form of a riddle or mnemonic device. Three different versions have been preserved: the oldest and longest is the Anglo-Saxon rune poem, corresponding to the older and longer Anglo-Saxon Futhorc alphabet, followed by the Norwegian version, and then the Icelandic. This passage is taken from the Icelandic rune poem. The full stanza reads: "Man is the delight of man / and augmentation of the earth / and adorner of ships."

is why it still adorns the forehead of the leading cow today when the cattle in the Germanic Alpine countries are first driven out to the mountain pastures.[24] And other symbols, such as Easter cookies and gable signs, point to the deeper meaning: when the rune is transformed into a human figure with raised arms, it is the Healer himself who begins to lift the sun high in the summer sky.

There are many interpretations of the Easter tradition in our legends and fairy tales, the most faithful keepers of ancestral beliefs. One tale tells of the six brothers who were transformed into six swans, and are then rescued by their sister and turned back into men.[25] Easter baked goods still depict the six-spoke wheel with the six swans suspended from the evergreen fir branch. Legends and fairy tales also take us back to a distant time when our familiar fairy tale images may once have been tangible reality, and when the name "Easter" still carried its full meaning. They still recall the maiden who is locked up in the chamber of an inaccessible tower with a single east-facing window, through which the young hero of the sun climbs in and leads the freed virgin to a spring wedding. This is how, among many others, the fairy tale of Sleeping Beauty has been passed down to us. The name Ostara,[26] which this symbol of the almighty life force once bore, still preserves the name and meaning of this ancestral legacy.

It also lives on in the customs that are nourished again and

---

[24] It is unclear what tradition, if any, this refers to, and there is no clarification elsewhere in the text.

[25] "The Six Swans" is one version of a story found across Europe with many variations, the core feature of which is a number of brothers being transformed into animals, usually some sort of birds, by their wicked stepmother, and their little sister rescuing them.

[26] A Germanic goddess associated with springtime and with the dawn. Her name in Old English was Eostre, and the name of the Easter holiday is likely derived from her.

again from the depths of the Germanic soul, and therefore have nothing to do with either "superstition" or with the superficial conceit of civilization of our time. It is the belief that on holy Easter nights, the divine omnipotence of life increases and permeates the whole of nature: the fire that burns on the mountains and the water that is freed from the ice by the new sun. Thus, in the holy morning hour, the women go to the flowing brook to draw the Easter water, which now itself contains all the healing, purifying, and invigorating powers with which the Easter sun infuses all of nature.[27]

An ancient and sacred mythical image! It reminds us of the women who sit at the fountain of the world and hold our destiny in their hands—of those women who draw our eternal values from the inexhaustible well of the Germanic soul.

---

[27] This passage refers to a tradition throughout Catholic Europe in which, early on Easter morning, women draw water from a local spring to be taken to the church and blessed for use in the Easter Vigil. This Easter water is said to have many healing properties for everything from skin conditions to diarrhea.

5

Brautweihe und Brautschmuck

BRIDAL BLESSING AND BRIDAL JEWELRY

For the Germanic, all the security of being, all the assurance throughout the change of ages and fate, lay in his fundamental understanding of the unity of the world, the unity of the inner and outer, of the individual and the general. Thus, the great processes of the world were to him great reflections of human life; human life, however, with its ascents, its high times, and its descents, was to him a reflection of the world-cycle in a thousand individual cycles— but in both cycles the same eternal and unbreakable laws ruled. So natural was the great unity of the course of the year and the course of life that it is still in our blood today, and our language still bears witness to this unity. When the sun prepares to celebrate its solstice, its "high time," the time when it stands highest and brightest in the sky, this especially is the time when lovers come together and set out on the path that leads them to the peak and fulfillment of all life. The wedding is a celebration of joy, a celebration of life itself, and if today the word denotes only the bridal celebration, this shows that all the festivity and joy of life is concentrated in this one celebration.[28]

How deprived we would be if we had to gain a sense of the world from the teachings of today's natural science alone, if we did not still live on the knowledge and wisdom that past millennia have left us! If we did not participate in the wedding every spring that the sun and the earth celebrate together, and that has always been the eternal archetype of the wedding between man and maiden! "It was as if heaven had quietly kissed the earth"—this has been the melody of every earthly wedding since primordial times; it has been the melody of all the truly pious joy of life that is consecrated by God, which passes on divine life from generation to generation, and which has never been completely drowned out by the gloomy concepts of sin and world-negation. We find evidence of this holy wedding and bridal consecration in the oldest pictorial depictions of our prehistoric times, in the rock carvings of the north. There the mighty, hammer-wielding sky-god, who lived in the form of our Donar, [29] himself stands before the bridal couple and consecrates them

---

[28] This entire passage rests on the fact that the German word for wedding, *Hochzeit* (pronounced HAWKH-tsite) is a compound word, the components of which, if given a word-for-word gloss, literally translate to "high time." On this basis, Plassmann attempts to establish a connection between the creation of new life that a wedding represents, and the life sustained by the spring and summer sun on the way to its solstice—its "high time."

[29] An older spelling of *Donner*, the German name of the thunder god more commonly known by his Scandinavian name Thor. *Donner* is still the word for thunder in modern German, and even the English word derives from the name of this ancient god, whose name in Old English was *Thunor*. As well as thunder and lightning, he was associated with protection of mankind from monsters, and, as a storm god, played a role in crop fertility by creating rainstorms, though this was understood to be only a side effect of his heroic exploits. His hammer is attested as being used for consecrations, including blessing a marrying couple.

with his weapon, the life-creating and monster-destroying hammer. It is the weapon he wields in the flashing lightning when heaven and earth celebrate their tempestuous union in the thunderstorm.

Even thousands of years later in a poem of the *Edda*, a giant-king commands:[30]

Bring the hammer to consecrate the bride!
Lay the crusher[31] in the maiden's lap!

---

[30] Referring to the famous Eddic poem *Þrymskviða* (*Thrym's Poem*), in which the giant Thrym steals Thor's hammer, and demands to marry the goddess Freyja in exchange for it. Freyja angrily refuses, and the gods of Asgard become desperate, as Thor and his hammer are the only ones able to defend Asgard against their enemies. They come up with a plan to dress a reluctant Thor up in women's wedding clothes to disguise him as Freyja, and send him to Thrym to "marry" him and get the hammer back. At the wedding, Thrym falls for the disguise, but is taken aback when "Freyja" eats several entire oxen and drinks three casks of mead, and when he lifts "Freyja's" veil to kiss her, he is startled by the fierce and terrifying eyes staring back at him. Still, the ceremony goes ahead. The hammer is brought out to be laid in the bride's lap, to bless the marrying couple. Thor takes up his hammer, crushes Thrym's skull, beats down the wedding guests, and brings his hammer back to Asgard.

[31] The name of Thor's hammer in Old Norse is Mjöllnir. The word most likely derives from the Old Norse verb *mala*, meaning "to crush or grind," as in grinding wheat into flour, for example, thus giving Mjöllnir the meaning "the grinder," or, more accurately, "the crusher." Even in modern English, the verb "mill" is a cognate with the Old Norse *mala* and has the same meaning of crushing or grinding, especially grinding grain into flour. By extension, then, the most direct and literal translation of Mjöllnir into modern English would be "Miller" (or its modern German version with the same meaning, *Müller*), a surname derived from the trade of crushing and grinding (milling) grain. In all likelihood, though, the true significance and use of the hammer is as the "crusher" of the enemies of man and the gods.

And another poet of the Middle Ages has the Virgin Mary say: "The smith from the highlands threw his hammer into my lap."[32] The war-hammer and the battle-axe were eventually replaced by the sword, and so we often find in old German legal customs the consecration of the bride with a sword. The traces of such sword carvings can still be seen on the bridal doors and bridal chapels of many old churches, just as they were previously attached to the bridal stones of the heath, on which the consecration of the bride was still performed into modern times.

We still know from several poems of the Middle Ages how such a wedding ceremony took place, and here the poets dwell particularly affectionately on the betrothal of a great

---

[32] A reference to the poem in honor of the Virgin Mary called the *Marienleich* (*The Lay of Mary*) by thirteenth-century Middle High German poet Heinrich Frauenlob, also known as Heinrich von Meißen. The "smith from the highlands" is a reference to Wayland the Smith (*Wieland der Schmied* in German, *Völundr* in Old Norse), a master blacksmith in Germanic mythology. According to the mythological account, Wayland is captured by an enemy king who cuts his hamstring to cripple him, and forces him to work at his forge. Wayland eventually takes revenge by killing the king's sons, carving their bones into cutlery and sending them to the king to eat with, giving the king's daughter a brooch made from her brothers' teeth and serving her a drink in a goblet made from his skull, then raping and impregnating her, before flying away with a pair of wings he had forged in secret from bird feathers. The character of Wayland has numerous parallels throughout Indo-European mythology, most obviously the Greek God of smithing, Hephaestus, or Vulcan as he was known to the Romans, who was also known to have a penchant for rape. Unlike Hephaestus/Vulcan, however, there is no evidence that Wayland was actually worshipped, though numerous other legends refer to magical weapons and armor crafted by Wayland the Smith. The meaning of the allusion in this poem about the Virgin Mary is unclear, and is likely just a literary device to suggest that she became pregnant through no action of her own.

and famous hero. Siegfried and Kriemhild[33] are married surrounded by a ring of friends and relatives:

They were invited to stand together in the ring
and asked if she would have the handsome man.

The *Nibelung* poet also tells a moving story of the betrothal of the doomed young Giselher to the beautiful Dietlind.[34]

But all these customs were originally identical, whether at the princely court or at the farmstead, and so it remained throughout almost the entire Middle Ages, until the old Germanic unity of life was destroyed from without and broke down within. The young peasant woman was queen on her wedding day, and the kingdom she took possession of was the farmhouse with its high seat at the hearth. For a long time, the young bride was led three times around the hearth fire or around the kettle hook, and right up to our own time, she enters her reign over house and farm by sitting down on the bridal chair. This bridal chair still bears signs of ancient significance, including the Odal rune,[35] the symbol of the

---

[33] Two of the protagonists of the thirteenth-century German epic poem, the *Nibelungenlied* (*The Song of the Nibelungs*).

[34] Two lesser characters of the *Nibelungenlied*.

[35] The *Odal* rune ᛟ, also called *othala* or *ēðel*, represents the /o/ phoneme in the Elder Futhark alphabet, and the /œ/ phoneme (pronounced something like the vowel in "foot") in the Anglo-Saxon Futhorc alphabet. Besides its phonemic value, the rune and its name also represent heritage, whether in the form of property, i.e., an inherited estate, or ancestry, i.e., nobility. In Modern German, the adjective *edel* means "noble," and the noun *Adel* means "nobility" or "aristocracy." Many Old English names share this same etymology, including Æthelwulf ("noble wolf"), and Æthelred ("noble council"). The female name Ethel is simply an alternate spelling of the Old English word for noble. The German name Adolf is cognate with the Old English Æthelwulf, and has the same meaning. The name Albert is derived from the Old English name Æthelberht ("bright noble").

sacred paternal heritage, which from then on the housewife must cherish and protect.

All brides originally wore royal clothing. The bridal crown is still preserved in many German regions, in the south and in the north. We also know it from ancient depictions, and among the royal adornments that the medieval painters and sculptors bestowed on their Queen of Heaven, the bridal crown, like so much else, is borrowed from Germanic reality. An ancient sign of the royal woman, as well as of the bride, is the "fibula,"[36] the golden brooch, usually set with eight stones. Its model and precursor is the Germanic brooch of ancient times. In the Middle Ages it was the sign of the princess and queen, but also of the woman from the free noble family, who alone was allowed to wear the "fibula" in the cities. Nothing is more characteristic of the old Germanic heritage, which was still alive in the High Middle Ages, than the Germanic bride in the "*Minnesang*,"[37] as celebrated by the old German poets as the archetype of femininity: she wears the fibula, the insignia of her courtly love. The same bridal costume also signifies divine love, adorned with the "divine insignia": the golden disc with the "seal of the world," as worn by the Aryan solar hero.[38] This again echoes the idea of the marriage of sun and earth, and when brides in Frisia, in Westphalia, and in Transylvania still wear this old solar sign, which is passed on from mother to daughter, this echoes the ancient and

---

The rune and the word it represents thus hold symbolic significance in the Germanic tradition, but the connection with a bridal chair is uncertain.

[36] An archaeological term for a safety-pin style brooch used to fasten a cloak, dress, or tunic at the shoulder. Among many European cultures, different fibula designs had different symbolic meanings, including signifying marital status and noble lineage.

[37] Songs or poems of courtly love.

[38] It's unclear what this passage or the "seal of the world" refer to.

timeless belief in the solar nature of life, of which woman and mother are the guardians.

6

Der Goldene Wagen

THE GOLDEN CHARIOT

His claws through the sky he draws,
With great might aloft he soars.[39]

Thus begins a "Dawn Song"[40] by Wolfram von Eschenbach,[41] one of our greatest old German poets, who hails the ascent of the sun as an eagle in the eastern sky. And in the greatest creations of our poets and singers, an ancient primal experience almost always resounds anew: it is the same experience of the new light that Master Ludwig von Beethoven echoed mightily in his much-sung and much-lived

---

[39] Translation of the early thirteenth-century Middle High German poem *Sine Klawen* (*His Claws*) by Wolfram von Eschenbach.

[40] A genre of German poetry popular in the Middle Ages depicting two secret lovers who, having spent the night together, must separate at dawn lest they be discovered. In *Sine Klawen*, von Eschenbach depicts the dawn as a fearsome winged creature ripping through the clouds to tear the lovers apart from each other.

[41] A late-twelfth/early-thirteenth-century German poet best known for his epic Arthurian poem *Parzival* about the quest of an Arthurian hero (Percival in English) for the Holy Grail.

verses six hundred years later:

> It comes and shines and beams at us from afar,
> and runs its course like a hero.[42]

The ancient Aryan experience of the sun hero, who steps out of his tent like a giant to run its course joyfully, is more of a daily experience for southern man, while the northern man, for whom light and darkness wage their own struggle on a larger scale, experiences it most deeply and enduringly over the course of the year. It pertains to the oldest and most intense experience of Aryan man, and thus all Indo-European languages have the same word for this eternal experience of the new light: Ushas opens up the day to the Indo-Aryan, Aurora to the Roman, and Eos to the Greek.[43] For the Germanic, however, Ostara, who comes from the same ancient sacred realm, has become, or rather remained, the goddess of the new light of the year; for the Germanic's experience of the world is rooted in the annual experience of the northern course of the sun. Thus, the name "Easter," or the old German "*Ostarun*," means "the days of the new light," in connection with the word "east." That festival originally hailed the sun at the spring equinox, when day and night dominate the sky in equal parts, but the day advances victoriously from then on towards its zenith. This annual festival was so strongly rooted in the customs of our ancestors that Christianity had to adopt its meaning when it placed the Day of the Resurrection of the

---

[42] Lyrics from Beethoven's composition "Die Himmel rühmen des Ewigen Ehre" ("The Heavens Praise the Glory of the Eternal"), based on eighteenth-century poet Christian Fürchtegott Gellert's poem "Die Ehre Gottes aus der Natur" ("The Glory of God in Nature"), itself based on Psalm 19.

[43] Ushas, Aurora, and Eos are the names given to the dawn goddess by the Vedic, Roman, and Greek traditions respectively.

Lord at the time of this festival of the resurrected sun, and that the name of the old pagan festival has remained alive with its original meaning to this day.

For what could speak more to the heart today, and what could give deeper expression to our longing for spring and the experience of light, than all the customs that are linked to the holy time of Easter—right down to the baked goods that the pious bakers make? They still form the ancient sacred symbol of the year-wheel in its cross shape into the dough,[44] partly related to the pretzel; they also form the yearly wheel with the six swans, the subject of a deeply-rooted fairy tale.[45] The four-part wheel itself is the symbol of the annual equinox, which still rolls down from the mountains in many parts of Germany today, wreathed in flame,[46] and, as a living image of the sun's course, heralds the new light and a new life to the fields and meadows. As early as the sixteenth century, Johannes Boehm[47] tells us about this certainly much older custom: "many who have never seen

---

[44] The shape he refers to is the sun cross ⊕, a cross made of equilateral arms, usually within a circle. Generally understood to be a solar symbol, the sun cross is commonly found throughout Europe as a decorative and religious motif, and is similar and related to the swastika, the "Black Sun" (*Sonnenrad* in German—literally "sun wheel"), and the Celtic Cross. The design is often pressed into the dough of baked goods, though the connection Plassmann draws with the shape of pretzels is dubious at best.

[45] See the previous chapter "Easter Fire and Easter Water."

[46] Referring to the tradition of lighting wagon wheels on fire and rolling them downhill, outlined in the previous chapter "Easter Fire and Easter Water."

[47] Johannes Boehm, sometimes written as Johann Bohm, Boemus, or Bohemus, was a sixteenth-century Christian cleric and humanist. His magnum opus, *Mores, Leges, et Ritus Omnium Gentum* (*The Manners, Laws, and Customs of All Peoples*) is considered the first scientific ethnographic study. This work is the source for the above quote about the custom of wheel-burning.

this astonishing spectacle believe that the sun or the moon is falling from the sky." The custom still prevails in the Odenwald, in the mountainous regions of Westphalia, in the Palatinate, and elsewhere.[48] The holy Easter fire, however, burns all over northwestern Germany on the mountains at night, when Easter Day gives way to the holy Easter night. In addition to the wheel, other symbols of the old sacred interpretation of the world have been preserved. In Attendorn in Westphalia, for example, the fire flares up around the sign of the man-rune;[49] and here, too, the old sign of the ascent to the annual height has maintained its old meaning. For in the runic calendar, it designates that quarter of the year when the ascent to the highest zenith of summer begins, when the "midsummer pole" is erected in the same shape as the old man-rune.

The wood on which this fire feeds is also of a very special kind: often it has to be stolen, i.e., procured secretly. But here and there it is still lit by a spark rubbed from two pieces of wood, set on fire with a pistol shot, or with the spark from striking stones together—a custom that even the formerly hostile Church has adopted for Holy Saturday.[50] Just as this fire is a symbol of the newly awakened life itself, it also serves to awaken life; people walk across the fields where the germinating seed is just stirring with burning logs, bundles of straw, or torches. Few people are aware that our own torch-lit processions, which today should once again be an expression of hope for new life and a new era, originate from these same torch-lit processions.

---

[48] Regions of western Germany.
[49] Likely referring to the rune more commonly known as Algiz, ᛉ (see discussion in the previous chapter "Easter Fire and Easter Water").
[50] The final day of Holy Week between Good Friday and Easter Sunday. A fire is struck from stone from which all the candles and lamps to be used in the Easter ceremony are then lit.

Leaping over the fire, which is done at Easter as well as at the Solstice fire, also carries this deeper meaning. It is a test of courage and at the same time of bold, new life, for all life requires boldness and daring. Indeed, one of our greatest myths has become legend: in the saga of the hero Siegfried, who rides through a wall of fire to awaken the sleeping bride to new life.[51] He is himself the ancient Aryan sun hero who awakens the light maiden Ostara, who sacrifices herself in a burst of flame to the beloved hero. Here death and rebirth are one, and rebirth from fire was probably the original meaning of these fires, as well as of the funeral pyres of our ancestors.

All these images that reflected to our ancestors the meaning of their world order—sun chariot, sun wheel, and new light—were still in the mind of the poet who wrote *Trutznachtigall*[52] when he wrote his poem three hundred years ago:

O beautiful Sun! O post so quick!
O golden steed and chariot!
O pure wheel from a pure spring
Shod with a gentle sheen!
In winter, the bright light
You give was lost
It seemed your wheel and your spring
Had frozen from the cold

---

[51] A motif in various Norse and continental Germanic sagas in which Siegfried (Sigurd in Old Norse) rides through a ring of fire to claim Brünihld (Brynhild in Old Norse).

[52] A collection of poems and hymns by seventeenth-century German Jesuit priest and poet Friedrich Spee, who was also known for speaking out against the witchcraft trials and hysteria of his time and the use of torture to obtain confessions. The title of the collection is sometimes translated into English as *Rivalling the Nightingale*.

7

Was der Maibaum Erzählt

WHAT THE MAY TREE REVEALS

One song that has become a popular folk song because it touches on a primal and elemental aspect of our people's nature sings of the linden tree that rustles by the well before the gate.[53] In this song, the old idea has become a poetic experience, which the tree, and especially the linden tree, is so closely related to man that a whole community has chosen it as its guardian spirit. The tree and its life are in close communion with the lives of those who planted it. The spirit of the community itself speaks from the rustling of the linden tree when God stirs its branches in the storm. Many a loving word is carved into its bark in the hope that—entrusted to the guardian spirit of common life—it will fulfill secret wishes and itself come to life. This is especially true for the secret wishes of those who entrusted their names to the bark. After all, according to ancient Nordic myth, the first human couple

---

[53] From the folk song "Der Lindenbaum" ("The Linden Tree") by early nineteenth-century poet Wilhelm Müller, famously set to music by the Austrian Romantic composer Franz Schubert.

was created from two trees,[54] where the eternal waves wash over the earth's shore and the All-Father's[55] breath[56] blows.

As sentinels of law and order, trees line the boundaries of the community; they protect the fields like charges of the highest knight and keep wrongdoers away. That is why he who harms the tree is punished like a robber or murderer: whoever cuts off the top of a green tree shall have his head cut off of its trunk, and whoever injures its root shall pay for it with his own foot. So goes the old peasant wisdom. But this profound folk wisdom can only be understood if one traces its deepest meaning: it is the sacred and inviolable life itself that is placed under such strict protection. In the life of the tree, the life of the many flows together, forming a living community like the trunk, branches, and leaves of the tree.

In some places, this primal feeling, which springs from a sense of nature that has become foreign to us, is still vividly perceptible. Our Low German fairy tale *Von dem Machandelboom*[57] tells of a tree that preserves the life of the murdered and gives them new life, and rustles its branches to comfort

---

[54] In the Norse Pagan creation myth, at least as outlined in the tenth-century poem *Völuspá* (*Seeress' Prophecy*), part of the Poetic Edda, the first two humans were created from trees: Ash (*Ask* in Old Norse) became the first man, and Elm (*Embla* in Old Norse) became the first woman.

[55] One of many epithets given to the Germanic god commonly known as Odin (*Woden* in Old English, *Wotan* in German), so called because he was responsible for shaping much of the world as we know it and giving life to man.

[56] Odin breathes the breath of life into the first humans to give them souls.

[57] A fairytale collected and published by the Grimm brothers, in which a boy who was murdered and cooked into blood pudding and fed to his unwitting father by his wicked stepmother is reincarnated as a bird when his bones are buried beneath a tree. The title is usually translated as *The Juniper Tree*, but occasionally also as *The Almond Tree*.

the desolate father and strike horror in the guilty murderer. Within a tree is the Völsungs' sword,[58] the sacred legacy of the clan, and also the knife of the two brothers, which announces by its condition whether the distant brother is well or ill.[59] Under the linden tree, the village community gathers for the Thing,[60] to which the living and the dead are summoned by solemn call, for an unbroken chain in the succession of generations winds itself around those who are alive, and those who were once alive but have not left the community.

Our maypole also has its origin in this sacred tree. When

---

[58] A reference to a passage in the *Völsungasaga* in which Odin appears as a one-eyed old man hooded and cloaked, and buries a sword called Gram ("wrath" in Old Norse) deep into the tree in the middle of King Völsung's hall, declaring that whoever can draw the sword will prove himself worthy of wielding it. All fail except the king's son Sigmund, who goes on to use it in many battles until Odin's magic causes it to break. Sigmund's wife Hjördis gathers the shards for their son Sigurd. Sigurd apprentices with the dwarven smith Regin, who forges the blade anew. Sigurd uses the reforged Gram to slay the dragon Fafnir.

[59] A reference to an element of another Grimm fairy tale called *The Two Brothers*, in which two brothers are given a knife by the huntsman who raised them and told to stick it in a tree if ever they go different directions, so that either one of them could return to the knife and see how the other brother was doing, because the blade would rust if things were going badly for him.

[60] A "Thing" was a general community assembly in Germanic society, in which an entire community gathered at a predetermined place of significance to discuss an important issue. The word, as well as the German/Dutch equivalent *Ding* and the Scandinavian *ting*, derives from the Proto-Germanic *þingą*, meaning "designated time." In English especially, the word has undergone a semantic shift and generally refers to an object, entity, or matter rather than a meeting, but the origin of the word is the same. The modern-day houses of government of Iceland (*Althingi*—"general thing"), Denmark (*Folketing*—"people's thing"), and the Isle of Man (*Tynwald*—"thing meadow"), and several others still incorporate this sense of the word "thing."

it dons its new green robe after winter's barrenness, when new life rises up its trunk and unfolds green and joyful, then the high time of the year begins, and with it also the high time of the community. The evergreen tree, which is decorated with lights during Yule, finds its counterpart in the summer-green tree of May; the spirit of community, which it symbolizes, celebrates its high time. This spirit finds expression not only in joyful and exuberant celebrations, but also in the will to defend the homeland. In addition to games and dancing, there is the great annual gathering of those fit for military service, which once brought the Franks together on their May field, and which today still calls the marksmen's clubs[61] to the King's Shoot,[62] which was once a very serious competition to determine the most skilled with weapons.

The sacred sign of the year was once hung on a linden tree. Indeed, there is a small town in Westphalia where a lighted lantern is still hung in the branches of the linden tree on May Day, and a mug of beer, the ancient Germanic sacramental libation, is poured down through the branches.

It was not always a felled tree that was chosen for the maypole, which was then erected in the middle of the village and decorated with a variety of symbols, with a large wheel and colorful flags. The living tree itself is its predecessor; it was once, and in some places still is, decorated to celebrate spring. The ancient Swabians are said to have had trees that

---

[61] *Schützenverein* or *Schützenbrüderschaft* in German, a gun club in the German-speaking world originating in local town militias, today serving more of a social, sporting, and/or historical function depending on the club.

[62] *Königsschießen* in German, a shooting competition at a *Schützenfest* (shooting festival, organized by the local gun club, but as much about music, food, drink, and socializing as about shooting), the winner of which will be crowned that year's "shooting king" (*Schützenkönig*).

they decorated with plaited branches and all kinds of treasures for the celebration. This idea in its most original conception plays a role in our national myth, which is the mythical expression of our national consciousness. When Emperor Frederick, or whoever else is meant by this, has returned from his mountain tomb, he hangs his shield on a barren tree, and it begins to grow green and blossom again.[63] In this way, the kingdom and the people on which it is built will blossom again when their time has come and they are given the leader who is destined for it. But the legend also tells us that until then, there will be a hard struggle, and that the powers of light and darkness will meet for a bloody battle at the birch tree, the tree of the great turning of the year and the world.

The great folkish awakening has also brought the custom of the Maypole back to honor in our country. Let us ensure that it does not become an empty showpiece that lasts for one day and is then forgotten again! Let us remember the ancient sacred roots of this tree, which grows from where the eternal waters of our nation gush, from the well of Urd.[64]

---

[63] Referring to Barbarossa, Holy Roman Emperor 1155–1190. Frederick Barbarossa (meaning "red beard" in Italian) was considered such a good ruler that he became a semi-legendary figure, and is said to sleep under a mountain (generally thought to be in the Kyffhäuser mountain range in Thuringia), awaiting the day when the ravens stop flying around the mountain, which will herald the nation's greatest hour of need, upon which he will awaken to save his people. The ancient king sleeping in the mountains to awaken and save his people is a motif of European historical legends, and can also be seen, for example, in the English myth of King Arthur.

[64] In Germanic mythology, at least as represented in the Old Norse poem *Völuspá*, Urd is one of the three Norns, female deities who are the personifications of fate, the others being Verdandi and Skuld. Her name is a cognate with the Old English *wyrd*, and Modern English *weird*, originally used in the sense of fate or destiny. Because fate is so often inscrutable, unpredictable, and unexpected, the

mechanism for the semantic shift to the modern connotation of the word *weird* seems clear. Urd is commonly called the "Norn of the past," Verdandi (cognate with Modern German *werdend*: "becoming") the "Norn of the present," and Skuld (cognate with Modern English *should* and Modern German *Schuld*—"debt, guilt, responsibility) "Norn of the future," but this may well be a misinterpretation based on their names. All three reside at a well (more like a deep lake than a man-made well) at the base of Yggdrasil, the world tree, and all are responsible for watering its roots and weaving the threads of fate. The three weavers of fate have equivalents in other Indo-European traditions, including the Roman *Parcae* and Greek *Moirai*, commonly known in English as "the Fates." They even appear as the "weird sisters" in Shakespeare's *Macbeth*, with the older connotation of the word *weird* that recalls the Norn Urd and the Old English concept of *wyrd*.

8

Von der Germanischen Landnahme

ON GERMANIC CONQUEST

An old Germanic idea has been revived in the world of ideas and the legislation of the German Reich: the land is more than mere property; it is the bearer of life, and is thus a high pledge entrusted to the cultivator by God himself for use and care. This basic idea explains all the customs and traditions that have been associated with taking possession of new land and the reclamation of old land since prehistoric times. These are acts of consecration that symbolize a covenant with the highest divine power, which reveals itself in the powers of earth and sun. These live on in the sacred fire that burns in the hearth and forms the center of all the land that is united under one owner. Thus, the patrilineal inheritance of the estate, the Odal,[65] is also a reflection of all the people's land and further a reflection of Midgard,[66] of the entire inhabited and ordered world. Just as the bride, on

---

[65] See the discussion on the Odal rune in the previous chapter "Bridal Blessing and Bridal Jewelry."
[66] The Old Norse name for the realm of earth inhabited by men.

assuming dominion over her household, walks around the hearth fire three times, so when the land was taken in ancient Iceland, the Norwegian conquerors circled the newly won land with a torch, or even lit great fires at the corners of the land itself, and it is expressly recorded that they sanctified the whole territory with this fire. In cases where the land area was not so large, a flaming arrow was sometimes shot over it. King Harald the Fair decreed that none of his men should take more land than he could walk around with fire in one day.

All these fire customs, however, are related to that great world-fire, the sun, which sanctified the land by its appearance over the new-won horizon. That is why the laws said that the fire should be lit when the sun was in the east, and that these fires should burn until nightfall. As a visible symbol of the marriage of the sun's power with the earth's power, a landmark was erected that was usually opposite the outgoing sun: in Iceland it was once an axe, the ancient sacred sign of Thor, the god of heaven and earth;[67] the landing place at the Öxarfjörður[68] was named after it. Everywhere, however, the custom was to erect a high pole, the top of which would be touched by the rising sun—often this was the pole of the very banner under which the victorious battle for the land had been fought. It then crowned the hill under which the fallen were buried, and the thought prevailed that their power, married with the power of the earth and the power of the sun, had become an element of the sacred soil itself, and thus communicated itself to the coming

---

[67] Thor (*Thunor* in Old English, *Donner* in German) is a god associated with thunder and lightning storms, as well as strength and protection of mankind. By the time the Eddas were written in Scandinavia, the weapon associated with Thor was unambiguously a hammer, but there is some evidence that earlier in the Germanic tradition it may have been an axe, or even a club.

[68] "Axe-fjord," a fjord in northeastern Iceland.

generations who cultivated the soil.

For it was very often the case, and in ancient times it must have been the case generally, that the land was taken from the burial mound of the fallen or of the leader, and that the center of the clan and tribal associations remained there from then on. This also explains the custom, which we find attested among the Saxons, of taking soil from the native land and spreading it on the newly-won land: it is the earth's power itself that is thus communicated to the new land, and the new settlers dwell on the soil of the old homeland. Many a later misunderstood saga has recorded this practice but turned it into a ruse, whereas it was originally a sacred and meaningful custom. That is why the Norwegian clans who crossed over to Iceland took the sacred earth from the holy places of their homeland with them to spread it on the newly built shrines. Perhaps the Swabians, who moved from the Spree and Havelland to the Neckar and Danube regions, also brought sacred earth from the ancient Semnon groves with them to Hohenstaufen, Tübingen, Hohentwiel, and wherever else sacred sites of the tribe were founded. The great idea of the unity of the German land becomes visible to us in such customs: wherever there is land consecrated by the blood and the graves of the ancestors, that is German land.

The idea that all land ownership is "received from God and the glorious blessing of the sun" is expressed again and again right down to the peasant wisdom of more recent times. The idea can be seen even in ancient times, when hints about people's lives and ideas were laid down in the rock carvings of the north; we find there the procession of the plough around the land, as well as the raising of the pole, which a later time expressly testifies to us. Thus, we may perhaps assume that the raising of the maypole, which takes place annually, and also the moving of the plough at springtime, are ancient customs that spring from the same world of thought:

it is the annual reaffirmation of the covenant that the ancestors once made "with God and the glorious blessing of the sun." And this type of idea may help us to interpret a monument left to us by the first historically recognizable, if tragically failed, campaign of Germanic tribes in Germany. It is the high and pointed stone at Miltenberg on the Main, on which a Latin inscription has taken the place of Germanic runes;[69] it tells us that this stone was erected between the territories of the Teutons, Cimbri, Ambrones, and Harudes.[70] Groups of these northern peoples settled in the Main region[71] during the great migration, and erected this high stone as a symbol of their conquest of the land, and their treaty.[72]

---

[69] Referring to the Toutonenstein, a boundary marker made of red sandstone dating to the second or third century AD, carved with an inscription in Latin letters that is still undeciphered to this day. The inscription appears in six lines. The first reads INTER, the second TOVTONOS, the third C, the fourth A, the fifth H, and the sixth is less clear but is thought to be an I. The single letter lines are generally thought to be incomplete, with the rest of the inscription missing, but an alternative theory proposes them to be abbreviations for words beginning with those letters.

[70] The Latin names given to various Germanic tribes.

[71] The region around the Main (pronounced "mine") river in south-western Germany.

[72] This claim is dubious, and is only one theory among many about the inscription on the Toutonenstein. Plassmann arrives at this theory by assuming that the C, A, and H are abbreviations for the Cimbri, Ambrones, and Harudes, which would mean the inscription reads "Between the Teutons, Cimbri, Ambrones, and Harudes." Plassmann assumes this refers to an alliance between these tribes to take the land from the Roman Empire. The Cimbri, Teutons, and Ambrones did once form an alliance against the Romans, but this was in the late second century BC, while the monument is thought to date to the second or third century AD. Thus, Plassmann's theory is plausible, but by no means widely accepted.

9

Sonnenwende—Sonnenschicksal

SOLSTICE—THE FATE OF THE SUN

This is the secret of blood and race: many thousands of years of experience flow into it, give rise to new experience, and sharpen the inner sense for all the thousand sources from which the lives and spirits of the ancestors still speak to us today. That is why we once stood as young wanderers around the solstice fire; that is why today Greater Germany lights the bonfires that are symbols for us of the elevation of life that our blood and our fate have set as our task.

This primordial memory is the secret of the magic of those bright nights when the fading red of the evening and the glow of the morning flow into one another; when the place of rising comes so close to that of setting that the summer sun's orbit appears like a high, festive gateway, which the lofty arms of the sun-hero arch above the summer earth. Among the images that stem from this primal experience, we still recognize the original and eternal meaning today: the marriage of the creative power of the sun with the maternal powers of the earth, and, fatefully placed between the two, the consecration of the human community, which is

indissolubly linked by blood, spirit, and fate. This lives on in a
children's song:

> Open the gate, open the gate,
> A golden chariot is coming.[73]

This song celebrates the old sun-hero himself. His symbols,
which were carved in stone, amber, and runic inscriptions in
ancient times, tell of his victorious journey to the heights of
summer. In Schleswig,[74] they erect the Midsummer pole, in
which the ancient man-rune[75] is preserved, for it is the sign
of the sun hero who raises his arms high to the summer sky.
There is hardly a festival in our summer season that is as
dignified and deeply folkish as the one that is still celebrated
every year in Questenberg on the Harz mountains at the
height of summer.[76] On a rock above the village stands an oak
trunk with a wheel-shaped wreath hanging from its crossbar,
which is replenished every year to celebrate the solstice. In
the early morning, when the first rays of the sun appear, the
village community gathers on the heights and greets the
rising star with horn blows. Then the old wreath is taken
down and entwined with fresh, new foliage, and the leaders
of the village community sit down in a circle, eat bread and
meat, and let the drink go around as a sign of the community
that embraces all. At high noon, the wreath is wound up, the
tufts of foliage are replenished on both sides, and the

---

[73] Lyrics from an old German children's song called *Machet auf das
Tor* (*Open the Door*).

[74] A region in the far north of Germany.

[75] See previous discussion on this rune in the chapter "Easter Fire
and Easter Water."

[76] Questenberg is a small village in the Harz Mountains of central
Germany. The tradition of hanging the wreath on the oak trunk
apparently still continued at the time of this translation.

beginning of the new half of the year is announced with shouts of "The Queste is hung!"

Anyone who has ever taken part in this festival feels a deep connection with those generations for whom the custom was once a true community experience. The wreath is a clearly recognizable symbol of the world-circle that encloses everyone and connects them to a community of fate that no one can escape, and in which everyone is ensconced. That is why in some places, girls weave wreaths of fresh herbs to throw on the trees or into the solstice fires—secretly hoping that their fate will also be rounded into its natural destiny in this symbol. Such a wreath once adorned the huge linden tree in Nordhausen,[77] to which the cobblers' guild, along with councilors and mayors, flocked during the summer festival to spend the solstice night. Even today, wreaths and crowns are fastened over the doors of the thatch-roofed houses of Lower Saxony on the eve of the holy solstice night.

It has remained a festival of light and fire to this day, and has become so again in recent decades. The burst of flame is its symbol, and bundles of straw and tar barrels on long poles are burnt and burning pitch wreaths are thrown into the water, for the liquid element receives the consecration of the sun on these holy nights, which from this point on is fated to descend into darkness again. The knowledge of the inevitability of this fate is what gave the Germanic peoples and their myths an inherently tragic feeling, but at the same time the knowledge also gave birth to the myth of the bright Balder, who must descend from the blossom of his sunny life to the dark Hel—struck by the spear of inescapable fate to which all living things succumb.[78]

---

[77] A town in the Harz Mountains of central Germany.

[78] In Germanic mythology, the god Balder (Bældæg in Old English) is the son of the god Odin and goddess Frig. He is said to be the most

For the Germanic, however, fate is not a dull, rigid constraint that intervenes in his own world from an alien realm. At the deepest level, we are all bound up with it, because the laws of the world are also our own laws:

> For conscience lives, and still its light divine
> Shall be the sun of all thy moral day.[79]

Thus, it is also significant that the greatest Germanic tragedy, the downfall of the Nibelungs,[80] takes place right at summer solstice: "It was upon a solstice that the great murder took place."

And the man who knows this fate, the grim and yet gladly brave Hagen,[81] begins the final battle with the cry: "Now we drink a toast and sacrifice the king's wine!"

The entire Germanic folk has had to live through such a fate again and again. And everyone who gives his all must endure those low times, a fate that is shared with the sun: those lows during which one is tempted to despair when everything fails, and when the best intentions are thwarted. And yet he will keep the spark alive within him, for the Germanic knows that eternal law of Dying and Becoming, of which his myths and symbols tell. He will not bow like a slave to a gloomy law that is incomprehensible to him; he will carry his light through the depths like a free man. For all

---

beautiful of the gods, with fair skin and golden hair. Loki's trickery leads to him being killed accidentally by his brother Höðr and descending to the underworld.

[79] From the poem *Vermächtnis* (*A Legacy*) by Johann Wolfgang von Goethe.

[80] A semi-historical Burgundian royal family, mythologized in the *Nibelungenlied* poems.

[81] A character in the *Nibelungenlied*.

light will make its way up again, just like the sun, of which it is a reflection. This certainty gives us the myth and custom of the summer solstice:

> And as long as you do not have this,
> This Dying and Becoming,
> You are but a dull guest
> On this dark earth.[82]

---

[82] From the poem *Selige Sehnsucht* (*Blessed Yearning*) by Goethe.

10

Sonnenheld und Heldensage

THE SOLAR HERO AND THE HEROIC SAGA

Beyond all historical events lies the mythical basis of our national life—and yet it continues to have a formative effect on our historical actions. Even today, we all pass through a stage of development in which the mythical heritage of our ancestors is a direct experience for us, more real and almost more salient than the demands of everyday life. There was the time when Siegfried, the bright and brave one, came to us as the eternal model of our essence, when we experienced his strength, his deeds, and his fate within us, when we slew the dragon with him, and read of his untimely end with fury and hot grief in our hearts.[83] Or when, later, the superhuman image of the Burgundian shook and exalted us, when we made the loyalty and disloyalty of Dietrich von Bern's companions and their deeds and sufferings the yardstick of our own friendships and adventures.[84]

---

[83] This passage draws heavily on references to the *Nibelungenlied*.
[84] See previous information on the origins of legends about Dietrich von Bern in the chapter "On the Sword-Dance and Sword Fighters."

Why are these figures, who seven hundred years after their deaths captivated German men and youth, still so familiar to us today, after another seven hundred years? What was it about Siegfried's dragon-slaying that still makes our hearts beat, we who have grown up with a natural science that has killed all the mythical beasts more ruthlessly than any hero ever could? The answer to this question is given to us by another science that deals with our own innermost nature: Indo-European and Germanic studies. It teaches us— for it is only a part of the science of life itself—why we are the way we are, why we feel the way we feel, and why this being and feeling has not changed in essence since the days of our forefathers, nor can it change if we remain what we are.

Heroic sagas and heroic songs hearken back to the primordial source of our people, from which we all originate and from which we draw our strength, whether we know it or not. They are a common possession, because they go back to a common original experience that was so powerful that its images are still alive today and trigger new experiences in us. All heroes who were worthy of veneration for us as boys, and still are today, bear the features of that primordial hero in whom the likeness of the divine gained symbolic form from the experience of world events.

Here lie the eternal roots of our Germanic experience of the Divine; they are firmly interwoven with our oldest experiences of the world, and everything that through the centuries of the last age has given our lives force and form, vibrancy and intimacy, is fed from these eternal roots, which rest firmly in our ancient, sacred land. Wherever the image of the battle-hardened hero has manifested as a historical pioneer of the nation, the image of the old Aryan sun-hero rises in him from the primordial mythical ground: it gives him his features, in which the handiwork of the Divine becomes clear, because every new hero who appears in the cycle of generations and centuries to lead the people appears as a new embodiment of this eternal archetype. These traits must already have been borne by the hero who for the first time in history led the victorious battle against Roman power: Arminius,[85] as the Romans called him, whose reflection we can recognize today in our bright hero Siegfried. Ancient legends are linked to his name: like that solar hero of primordial times, he grows up in the dark cave of winter to increase his power by divine strength and to prepare the way for new life. That is why, in the dark cave with the dwarves, he himself forges the sword with which he will win the decisive battle against the dragon.[86] We know now that the sword of iron was once made of bronze in earlier times, and that in even older times it was the stone axe that the sun hero wielded, and with which he blasted the capstone of the barrow, just as Thor shatters the stone giants of winter with his hammer. A barrow near Bremen has handed down to us a five-thousand-year-old depiction of this hammer-wielding

---

[85] Arminius, or Hermann in German, was the son of the prince of the Cherusci, a Germanic people allied with Rome. In AD 9, at the infamous Battle of Teutoburg Forest, he betrayed the Romans, leading three full legions into an ambush in which they were destroyed and their symbolically important eagle standards captured. After this unprecedented military disaster, the Romans withdrew from Germania, and the border of the Roman Empire never again expanded beyond the Rhine river. Arminius remains a folk hero to the Germans over two thousand years later.

[86] The suggestion here is that Arminius' time spent living in Rome, being immersed in the language and culture of his enemies, and training with the Roman military, mirrors Siegfried's time spent apprenticing as a blacksmith with the dwarves. It was during these time of quiet suffering that both heroes forged the weapons—physical for Siegfried, mental for Arminius—that they went on to use to defeat their greatest foes.

sun-hero.[87]

When, after the invasion of a foreign world over a thousand years ago, the expression of the Germanic experience of the Divine found refuge in the workshops of woodcarvers and stonemasons, the Germanic heroic saga faithfully preserved the old heroic spirit and recognized it again and again in the great leaders of its own time. Alongside the first liberators from Rome's superiority came the figures of the great migration period, above all the Gothic hero Dietrich von Bern. He, too, was adorned with the deeds and sufferings of the sun-hero, he fought with the dragon, he, too, found the sword in the dark dragon's lair that opened the way to the light, and he, too, was given sun-like eyes that reveal the divine spark, and that blaze like flashing lightning in anger. The legends hold that at the end of his earthly life he entered the stone house of the ancestors on a black horse, in order to return from it one day in the great final battle for the victory of life. And wherever a king or an emperor knew how to fulfill the longing of his people for freedom and justice, he took on the features of this primordial role-model, and the people awaited the return of the one who was the archetype of their own universal law.

In the oldest Germanic writings, he is the "god in the waters" who, according to the worldly experience of the ancient northern peoples, annually rises again from the floods of the sea to new life and new deeds. He is still depicted on a Germanic gravestone that his companions once set for a dead hero on the Rhine. Many an old legend tells us that the dying hero sought the sun with his eye, imbued with the knowledge that an old German poet put into words:

---

[87] Possibly a reference to the Neolithic stone barrow in Uelzen, though the claim about a depiction of a hero is ambiguous.

Were not the eye made to receive the rays of the sun,
It could not behold the sun;
If the peculiar power of God lay not in us,
How could the godlike charm us?[88]

---

[88] From the poem *Wär nicht das Auge sonnenhaft* by Goethe.

11

Das Heilige Brot

THE HOLY BREAD

As children, we all knew the legend of the proud Frau Hitt, who neglected and mistreated the bread, and was turned into a huge stone for it. As in most German legends, a myth from the distant past lives on in this one; from the time when in Midgard, in the god-protected world of man, bread was sacred as the bearer of life and salvation. Whoever tampered with it had to return to Utgard,[89] to the desolate world of the stone giants, where there was no bread and no life, without the sacred protection of the tribe.

An age that values life according to stock market prices has almost forgotten this ancient myth; only the most faithful guardians of unconscious good, the farmers and the children, still know of it. And yet, for the perceptive eye, it hearkens back to that ancient time when man and woman first prepared their place in the barren soil of the grain crop with the stone hoe, which was both cradle and grave for the grain

---

[89] Utgard (literally, "Outyards") is a desolate realm at the edge of the world in Norse cosmology.

in which life dwelt. From clearing to clearing it was carried on, it began its triumphal procession across the Marches, and wherever it took root, the God of salvation brought settlement and peace with him into the land. Thus, grain and bread became a symbol of the life-giving world spirit itself. Under this image, the eternal law of dying and becoming was understood, which also applies to man, inevitable and comforting at the same time. The myth of world events was also the myth of bread, which repeats those events in ripening and passing away. The spirit in the grain carries the holy spark of life through the ice age of winter and makes it rise again in spring. It carries the life of human beings, which is so closely bound to it that life is no longer conceivable without it.

"*Heilig*"[90] is the Germanic word for everything that supports and promotes life. Bread is sacred when it is scattered as grain in the field; it is sacred when it is scythed for harvest, when it is milled, and when finally it is consumed. Thus, the sky-God and his earthy consort are manifest in the image of the holy bread. It is the high time of the year when high heaven, with its solar power, lovingly embraces the motherly earth to produce the bearer of life: "Hail, Earth, mother of man. Grow great in God's embrace, fruitful to nourish mankind."[91]

This is how the Germanic ancestors greeted the "holy wedding," that was also the time of the human wedding. In the time of ripeness, a blessing procession walked around the

---

[90] Holy, sacred.

[91] From a ritual called *Æcerbót* ("Field Remedy"—*Æcer* refers to an acre of land), recorded in an Anglo-Saxon manuscript in the early eleventh century, but likely dating back much further. *Æcerbót* is an elaborate fertility ritual to heal unproductive land, evidently still very pagan even when the manuscript recorded it, but incorporating Christianized elements as well.

fields, commanding all land to the holy peace of God, and even in the Middle Ages, the ploughing farmer was under special legal protection. And finally comes the time of death, which here is a sacrificial death in the truest sense, when the reaper mows down the waving stalks that must serve life through their death. This is the basis of the ancient myth of the sacrificial death of the god: that is why the god of the harvest, of grain and bread, is also the god of the mown-down warriors, the ancient Wotan, who opens the way for life when he destroys life.[92] As a sign of his continued life, the farmers still leave the last sheaf in the field; it is destined for Wodan's horse, or it is called Wodan itself, because in it the divine life lives on symbolically. In the same vein, some grain was given to the dead in the grave. The room of the house in which the grain was kept was a sacred space, and in the Germanic hall was the sanctuary in which the divine life itself dwelt.

Ancient myths of kindred peoples tell us of the suffering and sacrificial death of the divine savior. The Greeks say of Dionysus, the son of Zeus, that he was torn apart and consumed by the Titans, but from the parts of the shattered Titans grew the race of men, who all carry the divine spark of Dionysus within them. In a very similar way, the Germanic peoples fashioned the myth of bread; Wodan, who lives on among farmers today, makes himself a sacrifice,[93] just as he takes the lives of men when life itself requires it. But he lives again in his transformations: in the sacred bread, as well as in the sacred intoxicating potion, as whose inventor he is

---

[92] Wotan/Odin/Woden is indeed associated with death, especially warriors slain in battle, though not so much with the harvest. Note that all spelling variations are preserved from the original.

[93] In Germanic mythology, Odin sacrifices himself by hanging from the world tree in order to gain knowledge of the runes, a motif that is quite possibly influenced by Christ's sacrifice in the Christian tradition.

honored, and in which he inspires and elevates man's spirit.[94]

The old grain spirit lives on in our folk belief under various symbols; whether it is the rye mare, who scares the children out of the grain to protect the holy crops, or the "rye cock" or the "rye woman," who are regarded as images of the spirit of life and also give their name to the last sheaf in various regions. The harvest cockerel, which adorns the last sheaf in many German districts and is displayed as a wooden image above the barn door, is a symbol of ancient mythical thinking.

That is why bread and all baked goods are sacred; even in primitive times, bread was given the shape of the symbols of the sacred realm: the shape of the gods or their sacrificial animals. At all the sacred turns of the year, such baked goods were eaten in honor of the life-giving deity. In consuming the bread, the symbolic union of God and man took place; that is why the tribe's dead also took part in it, to whom the "All Souls' Bread" is still given today at the feast of the dead, for they too are still under the great law of the universe.

That is why farming is noble and the highest obligation: the farmer is the keeper and guardian of the holy bread in which the divine lives. Reverence for the holy bread is reverence for the laws of life, to whose immortality it bears witness.

---

[94]Among his many other attributes, Odin is associated with "the mead of knowledge/poetry." Indeed, poetry and knowledge are closely related, as poetry was the principal vehicle for transmission of spiritual lessons and mythology. The mead of divine inspiration, Odin's lust for wisdom, his association with blind battle-rage and death, all have in common an element of transcendence of one's self and the mundane. The root of his name derives ultimately from Proto-Germanic *wōdaz*, which meant rage, fury, or manic inspiration—the modern German word *Wut* (rage) has the same etymology. Thus Odin is the patron deity both of poets and artists seeking inspiration, and of "Berserkers" seeking to go out of their minds and enter a blind rage and bloodlust before battle.

12

Der Geist im Korn

THE SPIRIT IN THE GRAIN

The ripe grain falls to the sickle, just as man at the end of his lifespan falls to the sickle of the great reaper in order to complete the cycle of existence anew. The spirit of life has taken on many different forms under whose image our ancestors conceptualized life and growth, which was given to them in the sacred grain and bread. Towards the end of its life, the spirit of the grain is simply called "the old one," or "the old man," "the Sheaf-man" or "the harvestman." When the grain has laid down under the pressure of the wind before being cut, they say the "old man" has sat on it. He also causes the grain to ripple, and when the sickle rushes through the grain, he retreats further and further into the uncut grain from the fallen swaths, until he is encircled and caught in the very last sheaves. Whoever mows and binds the last sheaf has caught the "old man," and must carry him from the field to the barn with his own hands: "You have the old man / And you have to keep him!"

In some regions, this old man is none other than "the

wode" [95] himself, the lord of the hordes of mown-down warriors, who has remained alive under his old name to this day. Here and there people still kneel down before the old man in the last sheaf, and even kiss him. This was a custom that was forbidden to the inhabitants of Prussian Warmia by a papal legate as late as the thirteenth century, but it did not do much to change the minds of the pious heathens. Thus the last sheaf of grain in the field becomes a man dressed in trousers, a tunic, a waistcoat, and an old hat, who receives the veneration of a good spirit. For even if it is claimed in Norway that this "reaper" lives invisibly in the field, and feeds on the farmer's grain all year round, this is only his right, for it is he who gives the grain its fertility and vitality. His figure is set down in the courtyard, the reapers form a ring around him and dance the round dance around him three times. Then the feast is held, which in Bavaria is called the *Niederfall*, and the barley man, the oat man, or the rye man is asked to take his share of the meal—in other words, a sacrificial meal in the true sense of the word. After the meal, the binder of the last sheaf takes the rye man in her arms and dances around with him three times on the threshing floor, and then the other sheaf binders do the same. Finally he is placed in a corner of the threshing floor and left to watch the feast until he takes his place of honor there until the next harvest. His power passes to the one who touched him last; this thresher is now called the "old man," is wrapped in straw, and has to carry a straw man on his back to the neighbor.

Perhaps it is an even older conception when the spirit in the grain is thought to be an animal, whether a pig, a goat, or a dog. When the wind blows through the rye field, one says: "there are wild pigs in the grain," or one sees the rye wolf or the rye dog. These spirits are good and evil at the same time:

---

[95] Derived from Wotan/Woden.

they make the grain grow, but they can also damage it. When the grain is mown, the grain spirit must retreat from each mown piece into the unmown one, and the reaper must be careful that he is not "rammed by the reaping-goat," or that the "rye wolf does not take him down." This is what they call it when a reaper suddenly falls ill during harvest time.

Today, the most widespread symbol of ripe and cut grain is the grain rooster, which was formerly killed along with the last sheaf in the form of a live rooster. It lives on as the "harvest rooster" and the "stubble rooster" in many other parts of Germany. In Brandenburg, the harvest festival itself is often called the "last rooster." A colorful rooster carved from wood is placed on top of the harvest wreath, which in turn is placed on a pole. The whole thing is carried home as an ornament on the last cartload and often nailed over the barn door. The wreath is the old symbol of the year-wheel, which as a symbol of the eternal "dying and becoming" encapsulates the entirety of life. This wreath is also placed on the pole in the rising grain field, often as protection against an evil grain spirit, the *Bilwis* or *Bilmesschnitter*.[96] He is supposed to mow long, narrow paths in the ripe grain field. He is thought of as a tall, bony man who wears a long-skirted cloak and a three-cornered hat and always has his hands in his trouser pockets. He usually rides through the field on a black billy goat; at the edge of the field he then takes off his right shoe and ties a small, very sharp sickle to the big toe, with which he mows the long narrow lanes through the grain.

It is easy to recognize in this *Bilwis* the figure known in many paintings as the "Grim Reaper": he is the reaper who

---

[96] *Bilmes* is a variation of *Bilwis*, and *Schnitter* means "cutter." The name *Bilwis* is of unknown meaning and origin, but the *Bilwis* is held responsible for unexplained patters or lanes of fallen sheaves in a field of standing grain.

mows people down like grain, and in all the details he can still be recognized in his original meaning. The sickle is equivalent to the scythe; the painted cross that he cuts into the field and that he himself carries as a sign has become an hourglass. Even keeping his hands in the pockets can be recognized, for, as a further development of the annual wreath, his figure stands on the stubble of the mown field with arms bent in a circle. We find the same figure, cast in bronze, as a burial object in the funeral urns of our Germanic ancestors. This "friend Hein" was not a frightening image to our ancestors, who knew about the law of dying and becoming, but the peace-bringing companion on the path of life, which flows repeatedly and eternally. And they recognized this deeper meaning everywhere: in the mowing of the stalks and the gathering of the sacred fruits of the field, as well as in the raging of battles, whose deeper significance was that they served the preservation and expansion of the Odal,[97] their arable land and living space.

---

[97] Here, this should be taken to mean "property" or "estate." See the discussion on the Odal rune in the previous chapter "Bridal Blessing and Bridal Jewelry."

13

Führer und Gefolgschaft

LEADER AND FOLLOWING

As long as there are soldierly alliances of men ready to fight, all martial activity will be characterized by the strongest bonds between a chosen leader and the men who are ready to follow him in every honorable deed, to battle and to the death. Thus, at the beginning of written German history, there is the description of the Germanic companions, which the Roman Tacitus may have recounted to a Germanic source:

The commanders rely on example rather than on the authority of their rank—on the admiration they win by showing conspicuous energy and courage, and by pressing forward in front of their own troops. . . . There are grades of rank even in these retinues, determined at the discretion of the chief whom they follow, and there is great rivalry, both among the followers to obtain the highest place in their leader's estimation and among the chiefs for the honor of having the biggest and most valiant retinue. Both prestige and power

depend on being continually attended by a large train
of picked young warriors, which is a distinction in
peace and a protection in war.[98]

This description contains all the elements that, in our
Germanic poetry, form the basic structure of all honor and
loyalty, and thus of any community of struggle: loyalty and
bravery between leader and retinue, and no less between
retinue and leader, for loyalty is only loyalty if it is always and
at all times mutual. This image was so deeply rooted in the
imagination and feeling of all Germanic peoples that a whole
series of words still bear witness to it today: leader, prince,
lord, duke and the terms "Truchtin" and "Thiodan,"[99] that are
no longer alive today, and for the retinue, "*Gesinde*," that
means "fellow travelers," "*Gesellen*," that means "hall
companions," and "Jünger," a word that has lost its original
meaning to a completely different conception. Originally it
meant the young men of the warriors' retinue, but the
Christian poets of the early German period knew no other
word to describe the retinue of Christ, and so the word and
the concept passed into a completely different world.[100] Not
only in legend, but also in historical reality, this leader
appears riding among his fellows and fighting at their head,
and often in the greatest moments of German history. King
Otto the Great rode into the great Hungarian battle on the

---

[98] From Tacitus, *Germania*.

[99] The meaning and etymology of *Truchtin* is unclear, but *Thiodan* is
the Old Saxon form of þeoden, an Old English word for a king or ruler.
The character Théoden in J.R.R. Tolkien's *The Lord of the Rings*
derives his name from this word.

[100] Here Plassmann engages in a bit of folk etymology. *Jünger* is a
cognate with the English word *junior* and means the same thing. It
is also the general word for the followers of Christ, whom in English
we call apostles or disciples.

Lechfeld as a true Germanic commander, as described by Widukind of Corvey:[101]

> In the fifth army, which was the largest, rode the prince himself, surrounded by exquisite swords from all the thousands and by battle-happy virtue, and with him was the victory banner, fenced in by dense army formations. The prince grasped the shield, he raised the sacred spear, and was the first to fly at the enemy, gloriously, as befits a king who commands men of war.

This host of armies, which surrounds the leader himself and does not leave the field alive when the leader falls, is a symbol of all solidity, all trust, and all security for the leader when he himself rides first against the enemy. Hagen, the archetype of the follower loyal unto death in the *Nibelungenlied*, issues the manly challenge of primordial times:

> "Twould well beseem," quoth Hagen,
> "The people's lofty lord.
> "Foremost in storm of battle
> "To swing the cutting sword."

Our historical heroes have always kept this loyalty to their men. Liudolf, the son of King Otto the Great, fell out with his father because he wanted to remain loyal to his young followers at all costs, and it is precisely for this reason that

---

[101] King Otto the First was a tenth-century East Frankish king and Holy Roman Emperor, famous for defeating the invasions of the heathen Magyars, and is thus recognized as a savior of Christendom. Widukind of Corvey was a Saxon chronicler and historian, and a descendant of the famed Widukind, the last pagan leader of the heathen Saxons and fiercest opponent of the Frankish king Charlemagne.

he has become a folk hero.

The greatest folk poetry, apart from the *Nibelungenlied*, the song of loyalty to men, and the Lay of Gudrun,[102] the song of loyalty to women, which for more than a millennium has been a symbol and example of loyalty to followers, is the poetry of Dietrich von Bern and his companions. The stories of him, the great people's king, were told wherever Germanic peoples lived: by travelers in Bavaria and Austria, by the Ostlanders of the Hanseatic League,[103] and of Westphalian merchants in the merchant's parlors of Norway. The theme, in various iterations, is always that of how Dietrich won over his companions after a hard struggle, how he remained loyal to them and they to him; how he lost the kingdom for their sake, and how he saw almost all of them perish in the heroic final battle with the Burgundian princes. And the tragedy of the Bernese originates from his loyalty to his followers: he abandons his kingdom before the false Sibich, in order to free his followers from captivity. Wittich, the unfaithful henchman, goes over to the enemy; but Heime, who is loyal in his deepest soul, Dietrich himself forces out of his circle through mistrust and forces him to go into the woods and wait for the day when he can prove his loyalty.

Here, too, Germanic folk poetry has recognized the tragedy of all living communities: that loyalty can come into conflict with loyalty, personal honor with manly duty, so that precisely the most loyal is misjudged. But this is the highest loyalty of all for the ancient poets, that Heime remains loyal to himself in the woods in order to stand by his leader on the

---

[102] The Scandinavian equivalent to Kriemhild from the *Nibelungen-lied*.

[103] The Hanseatic League was a medieval confederation of trading cities, especially port cities along the coasts and major rivers of Northern Europe, from the late thirteenth to the seventeenth century.

day of justice and to put the real traitor to the sword.

The basic forces of Germanic nature always remain the same in the German nation. Wherever a new living order was formed, it was based on mutual loyalty between leader and followers, and on the justice that prevails over both. Every community that rests on this foundation is indestructible; when this foundation is shaken, it is fleeting.

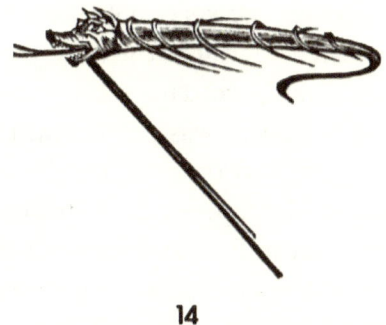

14

Die Heilige Fahne

THE HOLY BANNER

There was no great venture in the life of the Germanic in which he was not aware of the close and unbreakable bond with the spirit and nature of his ancestors. Their life was his life, his deeds were their deeds, and in his highest development of strength, in battle and war, he felt more than anywhere else their immediate proximity, indeed the complete oneness with them and their heroic spirit. From this knowledge of the unity of the living being across generations his symbols arose, and above all others the symbols of war and battle.

On the burial mounds of primordial times, which contained the bones of the ancestors in stone chambers, there stood as a mark and sign a pole carved from sacred wood, which is the symbol and seat of life for the nature-oriented northern man. It is not only a dead sign, but a living bridge from the world of mother earth to the over-world of the bright sky, in which the sun runs its course, and in which deeds are done, in which the dead of the clan and the people have their share, just as they participate in the spirit and the blood of those who perform these deeds. These signs were charged with divine power, both earthly and solar, connecting the dead who wait in the kingdom of heaven with the men who act in Midgard. This sacred sign, charged with divine and ancestral power, was carried into battle as a field banner; the young crew protected it with shield and spear and felt the power of victory emanating from it, for the power of the ancestors lived in it, and it was the belief in victory itself that was embodied in it. Until deep into the Middle Ages, battle was an arranged meeting with the enemy; thus the banner was set up on the agreed field and the shield wall was formed around it, where the commander of the army himself stopped and where the war god made his decision.

This field sign was crowned with a symbol of victory; in Germany it was usually the golden eagle, which still accompanied our German kings of the Middle Ages into war, and which had already been wielded by the Saxons one and a half millennia ago, when they advanced victoriously and extended their reach deep into Central Germany, and across the sea to Britain. Where they had won new land, they planted the sacred sign on the battlefield facing east, towards the rising sun: this was how ancestral spirit and ancestral power were transferred from the graves of the homeland into the newly won soil, and the omnipresent solar power consecrated the soil of the new homeland. For it was from the sun that the Germanic took his land, as many peasant legends of later times still tell us; but in the sacred field sign it married with the earth's sacred power, the maternal element, from which Donar, the old god of the Germanic peasant-warriors, was also nourished, as the Edda tells us. The eternal order of the universe united in it with the law of blood and soil, which is the original basis of all sacred tribal laws. And this was the ultimate meaning of all Germanic struggle: to live according to the law of the ruling sun, and at the same time to be firmly rooted in the power of the earth, in which the power of many thousands of ancestors resides.

This standard, which was firmly fixed in the ground, was later called the "stand-hard," meaning something that stands firmly, and from this our word "standard" is formed.[104] Today, as in prehistoric times, it denotes the standard of a warrior troop and its leader and the symbol of an unbreakable fighting community. The storming individual units, however, which plunged with sword and spear into the throngs of the enemy, carried a special standard, the storm flag with the long red bunting. It, too, originated in ancient times: the war spear of Wodan is its archetype. As a sign that the decision rested with him, the unfathomable power, a red cloth was tied to the shaft, which was probably once soaked in the blood of the warriors themselves. It was the sign that all those who followed it had consecrated themselves to death and accepted life, if it remained with them, as a new gift from the war god. But in this readiness for death lay the highest elevation of life for the Germanic who was prepared for war.

In the old Reich[105] it was the highest prerogative of the Swabian army to carry such a flag in front of the imperial army, in which the German confidence in victory and readiness for death was always embodied. Time and again, the flag had to be pulled out from under a mountain of men who had died defending it: whether it was the raven banner of the Normans, the banners of the German knights, or the flags of Prussian and German battalions. When the Germanic warrior today still swears his oath of allegiance to the flag, as did the warrior of ancient times, the old, sublime ideal lives

---

[104] This etymology is essentially accurate. Specifically, the English word "standard" and German *Standarte/Standort* derive from the Frankish word *Standahard*.
[105] The *Zweites Reich* (*Second Empire*), the *Kaiserreich* of Bismarck's era.

on in it: the spirit of the ancestors and their soldierly deeds reside in the standard; the spirit of the warrior community itself resides in it, which outlasts death, for the flag is more than death. That is why the flag, soaked with the blood of slain warriors, is forever the mythical rallying point of both living and dead warriors.

15

Der Heilige Speer

THE HOLY SPEAR

Among the national treasures of the Old Reich, which have
returned to their original place in the imperial city of
Nürnberg after an absence of one hundred and fifty years, the
most revered treasure is not the precious golden crown,
venerable as it must be to all Germans, but the iron spear tip
that the old king's spear bore. It is the oldest emblem of
Germanic leaders and kings, who displayed the emblem of
their rule not in the form of a golden crown, but the
victorious spear. This rule, however, was of divine origin, and
the sacred spear in which the rule was symbolized was itself,
in the true sense of the word, the emblem of the all-powerful
and victorious god who appears in later Germanic times as
the Father of the Fallen[106] and All-Father Wodan. Originally it

---

[106] In the original German, the term used here is *Walvater*, a
Germanisation of the Old Norse *Valfǫðr*. The stem *Val-* means "fallen"
or "slain," and is the same root that forms the word *Valhalla* (hall of
the fallen/slain). Odin is associated with death, especially death in
battle, and half of the fallen warriors, likely including all those who

may have been the Germanic sky god Tiu, whose name is used in the runic series to designate the spear-shaped rune.[107] If, therefore, our kings and emperors derive their rule from divine right, this is not merely an invention of the medieval Church; it is a continuation of the ancient Germanic idea that all human and earthly order should be a reflection of the great order of heaven and the universe.

In ancient Germanic times, as Tacitus reports, the leader

---

have devoted themselves to him, enter his retinue when they die. As the passage above attests, he is also associated with the spear.

[107] German *Tiu*, Old Norse *Tyr*, and Old English *Tiw* is a god associated with justice and counsel. Tuesday is named after him. The name comes from the Proto-Germanic *Tiwaz*, which itself derives ultimately from the Proto-Indo-European *deywós*, meaning "celestial/heavenly one." The Latin word for god, *deus*, also derives from *deywós*. In the Scandinavian tradition, Tyr can simply mean "a god," and can refer to Tyr as a particular deity, or any other god. Epithets for Odin, for example, include Sigtyr (god of victory) and Hangatyr (hanged god). The Sky Father (Indo-European *Dyéus ph₂tér*) is generally the chief deity in Indo-European religions: Jupiter derives directly from, and is a cognate with, *Dyéus ph₂tér*, as is the *Dyauspitar* of the Vedic tradition, and Zeus comes from *Dyéus*. Despite the apparent similarity of his name, Tyr himself is not the Sky Father: this role is filled by Odin. Indeed, Tyr is mentioned only a handful of times in the Scandinavian sources, and seldom if ever portrayed in the material culture of the continental Germanics. Tyr may have originally had another name that is lost to us, and the general epithet for any deity may have been extended to him, but he is not the Sky Father or chief deity in the Germanic tradition. Plassmann's speculation that the role of All-Father may have been filled by Tyr at one time is based on an idea that once held some traction in the relevant scholarship that Tyr was once the most important and chief Germanic deity and was supplanted by Odin only later, but evidence for this is very slim, and rests mostly on the assumption that due to his name he must have once been the *Dyéus ph₂tér*, but this line of reasoning is no longer generally accepted. As for Plassmann's speculation about the "spear-shaped rune," he is referring to Tiwaz ᛏ, which phonetically represents the /t/ sound, and according to the rune poems is named after Tyr.

lent the young follower the horse and the "bloody, victory-bringing spear." This too was a transfer of the leader's inherent power to rule and win to the young warrior. Thus the old Germanic images depicted Wodan and his representative, the army commander, predominantly with shield and spear, and the great Gothic king Dietrich von Bern, on the equestrian statue that once stood in Rome and was brought to Aachen by Emperor Charles, wields the spear as a sign of his kingship. The sacred spear was among the royal insignia that the dying King Conrad had his brother Eberhard deliver to Henry, the formerly hostile Duke of the Saxons, in AD 919: thus the ancient royal insignia is associated with one of the greatest deeds in German history. King Henry himself, who renewed the old East Frankish Empire with its Germanic roots, is depicted on his seals with spear and shield. The spear he wielded, which is still preserved today among the imperial regalia, was of course made by another Germanic people, but it is precisely this that reveals its origin in the common Germanic past.

In 922, the Lombard dukes had given the spear of the Lombard kings to King Rudolf II of Burgundy as a sign of their rule over the Italian Lombard kingdom. Four years later, this spear was delivered by Rudolf to King Henry, who thus symbolically extended his rule over the old Burgundian kingdom; the spear has since become the sign of German kingship in general. The Lombards themselves had adopted this royal spear from their distant Germanic prehistory; we repeatedly hear of it as the symbol of the divine calling of their rulers. Thus, on one occasion during an election of two kings, the right king was determined by the fact that a falcon perched on his spear. King Authari[108] extended his rule to

---

[108] A king of the Lombards (or Langobards), a Germanic people who settled in northern Italy in the sixth and seventh centuries AD.

lower Italy; he touched a pillar standing in the Strait of Messina with the king's spear, thus marking the boundaries of his rule. The legend of the Frankish King Otto I reports something similar: he is said to have hurled his spear into the Ottesund in the north of Jutland, thus marking the border of his empire.

But we know with certainty from history that King Otto wielded the sacred spear of the Germanic kings in the greatest and most decisive battle of his life, in the battle of Lechfeld on August 10th, 955. After a courageous address to the men of his retinue, he seized the shield and the sacred spear and was the first to charge against the enemy, who were beaten to total annihilation in this battle and driven forever from German soil. He may have kept the spear in his palace at Magdeburg, which he built, and thus the ancient Lombard royal sign returned to the vicinity of the original home of this people, after having been wielded successively by Lombard, Burgundian, and German kings—a testament to the permanence of Germanic essence throughout the turns of history. In 1002, King Henry II, the last Saxon king, took over the German kingship with the holy spear at Mainz.

A little later, the memory of the origin of Wodan's spear began to fade; ecclesiastical legend associated it with St Maurice, and still later it was said to be the spear with which Longinus, the Roman centurion, had pierced Christ's side on the cross. In the tenth century, an iron nail had been inserted into the spear blade, which was said to have pierced the right hand of Christ on the cross. The penetration of Christian ideas reshaped Germanic tradition, but even this blood-stained nail still reveals a dark memory of the "bloody, victory-bringing spear" of Germanic prehistory. And in Wolfram Eschenbach's *Parzival*, the spear soaked with the blood of the king is carried before the new ruler in the Grail

Castle. King Henry IV,[109] who had to defend the independence of the German Empire against the papacy all his life, had the tip of the spear bound with a broad silver band, to which Emperor Charles IV[110] added a golden band.

In a document from 1246, the holy spear is called the "spear and nail of our Lord"—the old spear of the gods has been completely incorporated into the world of Christian thought. But beneath this exotic shell we have long since rediscovered the Germanic core.

---

[109] King of Germany and Holy Roman Emperor from AD 1084–1105.
[110] Holy Roman Emperor, AD 1355–1378.

16

Sippe und Sage

TRIBE AND SAGA

Generation after generation once inhabited and cultivated
the soil of Germania in an unbroken chain, buried their dead
in graves of stone or in cremation urns, and pondered the
meaning of this life, which they lived with joy and strength
and in awe of the unfathomable, and which they gladly would
risk when the pressing need of the tribe or the people
demanded it. For many thousands of years, one member of
the tribe passed on the goods of life to the next; not only the
sacred grain of bread, which they revered as the visible sign
of life preservation, but also the goods of the soul and the
spirit, which, as the fruits of experience and knowledge of the
world, had grown over centuries into myth and folktale, into
allegory and legend. Until, in the time of the great twilight of
the nations, mighty armies came from the south to substitute
their law for those of their homeland, and the native
pantheon for their own. A superior leader gathered the
people together and met the enemy forces head-on, and for
a long time, perhaps more than a thousand years, people sang
of this leader who, through his victory, restored the peace of

the people and their clans.[111]

But another time came, more evil than the last: foreign armies came again, but this time it was their own tribesmen who led them, and in their wake came foreign men with other teachings, who no longer knew anything of all that had grown from their native soil. The ancient, holy world of the native traditions gave way and retreated into the darkness of the forests and the barren heaths. And ultimately it found refuge only in the souls themselves, which remained the same as in primordial times, and in what people told each other beside the crackling fire, and in the winter weaving cellar, and by the whirring wheel in the spinning rooms.

And with that, Lady Saga had returned to where her real home was: to the living circle of the successions of generations in which the sacred grain of bread and the living grain of tradition were passed on to children and children's children, in a life-giving and life-sustaining way. While the men and women in the prime of life perform the duties of active life, ploughing up heaths and clearing forests, the ancestors know the ancient, deep undertones that form the eternal accompanying melody of this active life; it is from them that the grandchildren who sit at their feet learn it, and who are at all times the most receptive to the ancient knowledge and faith and to the wonders that the world reveals to those who know its deep and ancient secrets. The elders and the youngest—they form the pondering and dreaming element of tribal life, which only through this addition becomes that mysterious primordial essence that we still sense today. Great ancestors still rest outside in the heath graves, and, as once they were in life, are now the sacred guardian spirits of the whole clan. They still know of the king in the mountain who took his treasures with him so

---

[111] Referring to Arminius and his victory over the Romans.

that no disgraceful quarrel over the treasure would disturb the peace of the clan.[112] They knew of the child at whose cradle the wise women came to bestow their gifts, and how the wicked woman then prepared a terrible fate for her, from which, however, the brave king's fearless son saved her.

And not only did they know all this, they also knew the places where it had happened. In the Mark,[113] they knew the mountain where once upon a time King Hinz was buried in three coffins with all his treasures. In Mecklenburg, there is a hill where the dwarves sat at a stone table and tended a bronze cauldron. On the Weser there was even a mound where a queen who had come from Norway was once buried; around her grave there was said to be twelve pitch barrels that burned for weeks. Such things and more were known and still are, and the "educated" had always shaken their heads at this "superstition" and directed the "stupid people" to other stories that were supposed to be far older and better attested than this spinning room gossip. Until one day a different sort of scholar came along, who had probably also heard the old stories and felt their wonderful magic, and they thought that perhaps the stories from this land were not so stupid after all. They excavated a mountain in the Mark, and lo, the king's treasures and his three coffins (there were three funeral urns) came to light. In Mecklenburg, a learned man called the peasants together, and when they really did dig up the stone table and the bronze cauldron, the peasants feared the wrath of the dwarves, abandoned their shovels, and ran away. Finally, on the Weser, a scholar, who was himself a man of the people and possessed their healthy reverence, also found the traces

---

[112] Apparently a reference to an obscure local legend of King (or Duke) Hinz or Hinze.

[113] A historical county of the Holy Roman Empire, now mostly within the province of North Rhine-Westphalia.

of the pitch barrels while digging and was able to determine exactly where they had stood. Now, little by little, the ancient wisdom of the people was seen with different eyes, and it was recognized that this wisdom was much more genuine and lasting than all the parchments that had been brought from foreign lands and extolled as ancient revelations. And it was recognized that other legends also have a deep, venerable core: for example, the legend of the great people's king who sits at the stone table in the mountain, and waits for the day when his people call him to their aid in the greatest need.[114] The entire German nation has come to feel so much like a single tribe that it has made this ancestor in the mountain an eternal symbol of the whole people and nation.

And so we were able to rediscover and correctly interpret the ancient, profound motif of the good spirits giving their gifts to the newborn in the cradle as wise women on a grave depiction in Sweden. The good gifts are the heritage of the tribe that is given to every newborn. The one evil gift, however, which is probably given to everyone in the cradle, must be overcome by a life of struggle, the symbol of which is the king's fearless son.

---

[114] See footnote 63 for discussion of Frederick Barbarossa, and the motif of the king in the mountain, in the previous chapter "What the May Tree Reveals."

17

Der Heilige Herd

THE HOLY HEARTH

In the oldest myths of humankind, fire has become the symbol of the ascent of humanity; as the keeper and master of fire, man is most visibly distinguished from the animals, who all fear fire. The mythical Prometheus, who brought fire from heaven to mankind, became the epitome of the forward-thinker who, in his battle with the forces of nature, won for them their most powerful ally: fire.

In the northern house of primordial times, the sacred fire blazed in the stone fire pit in the middle of the living room, the only source of warmth, light, and comfort when the northern winter night seemed to have devoured the great, fiery star of the day. The sacred fire was the carefully cherished symbol and guarantor of the light of the world, which had to fight in the underworld against lindworms and fiends; as far as it spread light and warmth, it enclosed life itself within its circle, and in this circle the ancient, eternal myth of the bright sun-hero and his deeds and sufferings may have been first composed.

It remained an element and symbol of life even in later

times, when the old dwelling house had extended far and wide in length, width and height; when it had stretched up on pillars of oak trunks and carried a huge, overhanging roof, in whose dim height the sparks of the crackling hearth fire flew, and through whose cracks and joints the smoke sought its way out. The fire pit moved to the upper end of the long rectangular house, where the clay, plank, or stone-floored part of the hall was, which in northern Germany is still called by the ancient name "Flett." The sacred hearth was the center of clan life, and from very old traditions we can conclude that originally even the ancestors themselves were buried under the hearth. The sacred hearth was the seat of the woman who was enthroned here as the queen of the house, just as the prince had the seat by the fire in the royal hall among his faithful, and just as the farmer's wife in Westphalia can still overlook and direct the whole house from the hearth seat today. She is, so to speak, the guardian of the sacred fire itself, and as the bearer of this task, she might also have become the guardian of the sacred fire that religious communities maintained as the centers of their worship of God. For the ideas and institutions of the service of the gods were transferred by the northern peoples from the narrower sphere of clan life, to the larger scales of the world and world order, just as the word "home" in the Nordic language denotes both the narrower setting of clan life and the setting of the affairs of the whole world.[115]

The custom of leading the young woman around the hearth three times when she moved into her new home has been preserved to this day, thus giving her dominion over the interior of the house. Where the hearth had been moved to the back of the house, as was usually the case later in the

---

[115] The Old Norse word *heim*, which is cognate with modern German *heim* and English "home," could mean home, realm, or world.

Saxon home, she was at least led around the kettle hook, which was a very special ornament of the house with its elaborate wrought-iron and its rich symbolic content. Decorated with its year wheels, sun wheels, and all kinds of creatures from the world of myths and fairy tales, it has preserved the tradition from the time when the sacred hearth fire was worshipped as the image of the great sun. This great parable used to be represented in the common custom of extinguishing all hearth fires far and wide with water at the time of the winter solstice, when, according to the oldest myth, the sun sank into the world's oceans, and then lighting the new fire with the wooden fire drill. Originally, twins had to light the fire in front of or underneath the large hall gate, and from this fire the farm owners from near and far fetched the new fire for their hearth.

This custom of renewing the hearth, which today still goes by the name "need-fire," was harshly repressed in the time of conversion, and yet it has survived under the old name right up to our century. It was closely connected with the customs of the solstices, especially the winter solstice, when the rebirth of the sun was celebrated in the rebirth of the fire. Then the "yule block" was rolled into the renewed hearth fire, usually the root end of a tree, and the tree of life and other symbols of the yearly cycle were carved into the soot on the hearth wall. This is where the world of man and the world of the spirits, who in the legends enter and leave through the chimney, come into closest contact; the Wild Hunter[116] also likes to throw his healing or sinister gifts down through the chimney.

All these are only variations of the ancient, sacred associ-ation of the hearth fire: it is the light-giving and warming

---

[116] See discussion of the Wild Hunt in the previous chapter "The Turn of Winter—The Turn of the Year."

center of the clan, the refuge of its life, and thus itself an allegory of the eternally living.

18

Deutsche Totenfeier

GERMAN FESTIVALS OF THE DEAD

It is graves that remind us most vividly of the life of ancient times. For our ancestors they were monuments of life itself; without them we would know little of the life of the ancestors, of their artistry, of their valor in arms and of their mighty strength—and above all of their insight and thought. Their graves are sacred places because they bear witness to the knowledge of the indestructibility of life, because the will to eternity manifests itself most meaningfully in the change of ages. Honoring the ancestor—that was the basic idea that set the arms of Stone Age people in motion when they rolled granite blocks from far away and piled them up to form houses for the dead, the like of which had never been erected for a living person. By honoring their ancestors, however, they erected monuments to themselves, and we stand in awe of the ancestors as well as of the descendants who were capable of such deeds. For what could move a person of the north, who has to struggle enough with the hardships of life, to make such a superhuman effort to honor the dead, if not a lofty and mighty idea?

Gone are the days when scrawny scholars thought they could explain such deeds out of the survivors' fear of the dead. A better knowledge of our folk tradition could have taught them better. For indelible, living, and real memory clings to the graves of the past through thousands of years. Stronger than the horror at everything that has to do with death and passing away, was the feeling that an indissoluble connection prevailed over all parting and passing away; that a constant mysterious coming and going prevailed in the eternal succession of blood, and established a firm relationship and an indissoluble bond between those who lived and those who had gone. This thought was at the center of all symbolic interpretation, which was expressed in the honors paid to the dead: no afterlife divided between hell and heaven, as in southern countries, but life in the circle of the tribe or of comrades in arms; the Midgard of our ancestors and its heroic supplement by the Valhalla of the warriors. And if the hero still needed purification, there was room enough for it here on earth, on the scene of the eternal heroic struggle. Legends, fairy tales and customs, the deepest testimonies of our true world view, offer abundant evidence of this.

The dead hero was also destined for new deeds in the "hereafter," that was usually meant to be a new life on this earth; that is why he was buried in the full adornment of arms, which is why his companions in arms rode around his grave and sang of his deeds:

Then about that barrow the battle-keen rode,
Atheling-born, a band of twelve,
Lament to make, to mourn their king,
Chant their dirge, and their chieftain honor.
They praised his earlship, his acts of prowess
Worthily witnessed: and well it is
That men their master-friend mightily laud,

Heartily love, when hence he goes
From life in the body forlorn away.[117]

This is how the Anglo-Saxon poem sings of the death celebration of the brave Beowulf. But the king who dwells in the mountain is henceforth the guardian spirit of the tribe and of the whole people, and even hundreds of years later the people know that a king dwells there, and what weapons or ornaments he has with him.

Germanic man imagined life after death as a continuous action and struggle. For once a hero and warrior had fallen in battle, it was impossible for that stormy force inside him to fade into nothingness; it had to continue to work, even if it was in the storms of great nature itself. Thus arose the great image of the wild army in which the souls of the departed ride through the air under the leader of Thor or Odin;[118] and it was not for nothing that the day of the leader of the dead was set for the end of the September, when the storms of the autumnal equinox begin to sweep away the withered leaves. Even when St. Michael later took his place, nothing had changed except the name. Throughout the Middle Ages, the great autumn gatherings fell on the great autumn *thing-day* of the old sword god.[119] The living and the dead were summoned by a solemn call to this annual event, at which court was held in the name of the law-keeping sword god.[120] The great bond that enclosed the place of the *thing* embraced them all in the name of the sacred peace of the law and the

---

[117] *Beowulf*, pp. 3169-3170, translated by Francis Barton Gummere.
[118] See discussion on the Wild Hunt in the previous chapter "The Turning of Winter—The Turning of the Year."
[119] See discussion on the *thing* in the previous chapter "What the May Tree Reveals."
[120] Likely referring to Tyr, who was associated with the sword, as well as with law and order, and thus the *thing*.

tribe.

Much has changed under the influence of foreign ideas, which has made us forget our ancestors from the dim past. Today, with the help of research, we have again reached the roots of our being, and only now are we able to appreciate how faithfully the people's minds have preserved their knowledge of these roots over the millennia. Above all, it is tradition that runs like a great axis through our conscious history: the legend of the king in the mountain who sits at his stone table, adorned with weapons, and as a mighty ancestor of the tribes watches over the salvation of future generations, only to emerge again at the hour of the people's greatest need.

19

Der Deutsche Roland

THE GERMAN ROLAND

In the barrows of ancient times, the ancestors of the great families rested in stone burial chambers or in clay urns. The grave was more to the descendants than it tends to be to us today: it was the place where the ancestral power was alive and flowed invisibly from the blood of the dead in the barrows. The trunk of a tree was erected on the grave as a visible sign of this ancestral power, which passed over to men and gods as "earthly power," the trunk as a symbol of the living tree, just as the resting place of the dead man was itself a symbol of the indestructible life force that rules in his race. In the form of this sacred post, the ancestor was present with his power among the living; at the touch of his emblem, it passed over to the living; whether he stood in the midst of the assembly as the supreme oath-witness at the *thing* and court, or he was carried forth as a banner for the army in battle. It guaranteed the iron preservation of justice and righteousness, or it brought about victory. For a single great bond held all the members of clan and people, whether they lived in the light or dwelt in the realm of the dead, and thus, even in later times, the Lord of Judgment delivers the dead and the living to judgment.

In this sacred post, the power of the earth was symbolically united with the power of the victorious sun under which the living dwell, and thus the land of the ancestors was united with the land of the grandchildren. When new land was taken for clans and generations of the people, the sacred ancestral post was erected on the won ground as a sign of the claiming of the land, and the ancestral power flowed over to the new land. Since the sun and the daylight have always been the guardians, the ancestral grave and the ancestral post became the center of the courts, and through them the sacred peace of law was visibly and tangibly embodied.

A foreign faith and a foreign law came over the Germanic land and brought foreign ideas and forms, which struck many an old sacred belief and custom to their very roots. But as little as they were able to separate us from our ancestors in terms of blood, so little were they able to uproot what had been created by the blood and spirit of the ancestors for millennia. Ancient sacred rites were transferred to the Churches; but the new *thing*-place, the steeple, took the name of that sacred ancestral and judicial pole among the Anglo-Saxons themselves.[121] The old grave signs made way for new ones, but the ancestral spirit was not so easily banished from the legal system. It lived on, next to its living counterpart, the court linden, which rustled above the stone seats of the jurors. It even invaded the church tower, strangely transformed into the image of a pugnacious saint

---

[121] Plassmann's contention here is that the Old English word *stīpel* (steeple, post, pillar) was also previously used to refer to posts marking barrows, and simply adopted to refer to the towers atop Christian churches. This etymology is unconfirmed.

standing on the pillar, like Patroclus in Soest[122] and formerly St. Maurice in Magdeburg.[123] But in some regions, such as East Prussia, it has also survived as a grave marker, and the living wood still tells us more today than the magnificent stones of the dead, which have come to us from a foreign world.

Originally, the sword of justice itself was hung on the judicial post as a place of legal peace, which is why it was also called the sword post, and next to it perhaps also the shield of the king, who had early become the supreme lord of the court. Since time immemorial, the Germanic people have worshipped the divine in the sacred symbol, not in human form, and so it was only in later times that the sacred wood was given suggestive human features, which point to the one whose power lives in the symbol. We know that in Scandinavia, the ancient Norse had already given the sacred high-seated pillars, in which Thor's power lived, a hint of a face. On the mainland, this transition took place much more slowly. But little by little, the ancestral pole with the sword became a sword-armed human figure, sometimes with a shield; since the Middle Ages, these symbols have been called "Rolands."[124] In most of them, the arms and sword, pressed tightly against the body, still hint at the original shape of the pole. Wooden Rolands, which have been preserved here and there in small towns and villages, still have the original shape, with only notches indicating a head, as the old grave poles

---

[122] At the Sankt Patrokli Dom in the town of Soest, Germany, St. Patroclus is depicted as a warrior.

[123] St. Maurice is traditionally depicted in a full suit of armor.

[124] The historical Roland was a Frankish military commander serving under Charlemagne. Roland can indeed also be used as a general term for a statue with a drawn sword and shield. Plassmann's claim that these actually originate from grave markers on barrows is speculative.

still show today. Those Rolands that hold the sword arm stretched out far from the body can be traced back to another basic form: the arm with the sword was originally a sign of legal authority, attached to town halls and law courts.

With the disappearance of Germanic freedom among the German peasantry, the old legal symbols often left the countryside for the cities, where they became witnesses to successfully asserted freedoms and rights for centuries. Thus emperors and kings, who were regarded as the creators of freedoms, were also placed on the old court post, such as the great Emperor Otto, who is enthroned as a horseman under a canopy on a high column in Magdeburg on the market square. Only in Westphalia, in the land of the "Red Earth," have the old peasant courts survived into modern times as the *feme*;[125] and the name "Red Earth" also explains the name of the venerable legal symbols, among which the giant Roland statue at the Town Hall in Bremen is the best known and most recognized, but not the oldest. "Red Earth" or the "Red Land" are old names for the sites of the courts conferring capital punishment, which were enclosed with a red thread as a sign of legal peace. From this enclosure of things, the "Redland" (*Rotland* in German), the name has passed to the old landmark

---

[125] The Vehmic courts, also called *Feme* or *Vehm*, were originally a system of quasi-vigilante courts among the peasantry of Westphalia during the Middle Ages. The proceedings and judgments were sometimes conducted in secret, and thus the Vehmic courts were sometimes called "the silent court," leading to death sentences that resembled assassinations. The bodies of the convicted were then hanged from trees along roads as a warning to criminals. In the Weimar era, various far-right paramilitary groups, especially the shadowy, esoteric-Aryanist, ultranationalist secret society *Organisation Consul*, conducted similar activities, holding secret proceedings, passing illegal death sentences, and carrying out extrajudicial assassinations against those they deemed enemies of Germany, notably including Foreign Minister Walther Rathenau.

in its center, which therefore has nothing to do with the name of the well-known Frankish hero. According to the old statutes, however, the aldermen of the *feme* court had to be elected "on red earth," i.e., on an old site, and since the Land of Westphalia was the land of origin and the last refuge of the *feme*, it was dubbed the "Red Earth" itself. In the course of the millennia, however, the original meaning of the ancestral symbol as the guardian of clan life has survived in some places. In Bramstedt in Holstein, marrying couples are led around the Roland statue three times after the wedding ceremony, and songs are sung:

So long as the wind blows and the cock crows,
Let there be dancing around the Roland,
When down the sun goes.

20

Die Geburt des Lichtes

THE BIRTH OF THE LIGHT

Nordic and Germanic faith has lived for millennia in symbols and in those who created these symbols. Symbols are more than ornaments; they are ancestral images of an innermost experience, imprinted in forms that speak mysteriously to the one who has blood from blood and spirit from spirit of those who once, in primordial times, created those symbols based on their experience of the world. That is why they still speak to us today, why they awaken in us that primordial experience that is unique and eternal, which is not subject to any psychology or evolution, because it emanates directly from that point of the soul where the human meets the divine.

This primordial experience is the birth of light. To the Germanic, everything that appears transient to us is a likeness of the great eternal, the All-Father of the world, of life, and of our being. And that is why dying and becoming are a guarantee of the eternity of being. Holy days and holy nights, however, are those times in which this eternal being becomes visible when death and life meet. In primordial times, on the edge of the Arctic, this experience seized and shook the northern man anew every year. When the sun, which had long since sunk into the darkness below the circle of vision, first flashed up again behind the southern mountains, above the southern winter sea, when the light shone in the darkness, he was seized with overwhelming joy, and a joyous festive season was consecrated to this rebirth of light. It was not much different for the peasant in the German plains and mountains: when the new light announced new life and new growth to him, he himself felt inwardly connected to this new life. The spark of life, rejoicing in God and in activity, rose up in him and lifted his soul towards action and work.

This primal light illuminated and enlivened the Germanic wherever he went to fulfill his mission. It shone in the youthful crowds of the people at springtime, when they went out to win new land for light and life; it shone in the warriors who walked their course resolutely like the sun, "joyful as a hero in victory." It shone on the bold Vikings, when they steered their keels across the dark maw of the sea for voyages across the world. And it shone for those German men and women who, far from an alien externalization, sought the divine in themselves and found it again in the "little spark" of which Meister Eckhart [126] speaks. The pious mind of our people has experienced the rebirth of light in many different images, and has written poems about it. One of the oldest and most beautiful is that of the newborn child lying in a golden cradle in the hill of the ancestors, which gives wonderful expression to the belief in the sun-like divine life in the clan. Another is that of the winter-green tree that preserves life through the night of the year, and lets it blaze in light on its branches. And a third image, often sung in legends and fairy

---

[126] A late-thirteenth-century German theologian whose central idea was the presence of divinity in the individual human soul.

tales, is the virgin with the golden hair, who is locked up in a dark tower, only to reappear after her imprisonment, radiant with new life. A tower made of clay is one of the most beautiful symbols of our Christmas season. It is decorated with the year-wheel, the holy Jul, and the heart, the symbol of Germanic divinity. At the bottom of the tower, a candle burns, the symbol of light in the darkness, until the great light on top of the tower is lit at the beginning of the new year.

This is how it may have once burned on the towers of our ancestors in primordial times, of which only a single scholarly report, but many legends and fairy tales, and especially these tower candlesticks still in popular use, bear witness. In this symbol, Germanic heroism and deep spirituality have found their common expression. They are still alive today in our German Christmas experience, which no foreign spirit has ever been able to distort or darken.

21

Vom Wilden Heeren und den Drei Wanderern

ON THE WILD HOST AND THE THREE WANDERERS

In the storms of the winter night, the Germanic experiences the work of almighty God. That is why Odin, the leader of the army of the dead, is also the lord of the twelve nights in which the wheel of the year stands still;[127] the nights between the solstice day and the Perchta's day,[128] on which

---

[127] Referring to the old Germanic month of Yule (roughly corresponding to December), which culminated in a twelve-day Yule festival, from which many traditions still survive today, having been incorporated into Christmas traditions. This period marked the transition between calendar years. The etymology of the word is uncertain, but it evidently had some connection to the god Odin, one of whose epithets is *jólnir* (the "Yule one," "Yuler").

[128] Perchta, Berchta, or Bertha is a goddess attested mostly in Alpine regions of southern Germany, Austria, and Switzerland, associated with the twelve days of Yule. She is said to have two forms: the "beautiful Perchta," radiant and white as snow, and the "ugly Perchta," wrinkled and haggard, or even a horned beast. On this basis, celebrations in the Alps often include a procession of beautiful *Perchten*, and one of ugly *Perchten* wearing frightening horned masks to drive away evil spirits. The "Perchta's day" (*Perchtentag* in German), which Plassman refers to is now the Feast of the Epiphany on January 6th.

the wheel begins its new turn. In this twelfth night, however, the wheel of the world comes to a standstill and with it the world order, and so the hostile Utgard,[129] the world of fiends and evil spirits, breaks into Midgard, the world of salvation and human security. The Germanic is accustomed to ups and downs; he is familiar with life and death, and he acquaints himself with the struggle against that other world, whose forest is the storming nature, but also his own heart. Thus he may experience all the more deeply that great upheaval that every year puts his ability to live to the test, and if he participates wholeheartedly in this decisive struggle, he will heroically increase the power of his own heart. He knows that when the All-Father roars on his white horse over trackless forests, tugs at the roofs, and blows into the hearth fire, the fire will gain new strength, and the sacred spark in his own breast is kindled higher when it shines in the darkness.

Thus he himself once formed a wild army with death-defying men, roaming the forests and, with flaming torches, booming drums and blaring horns, feeling completely at one with that eternal army that moves with the clouds in the winter storm, awakening the sleeping nature and kindling new fire in the hearths and the hearts of bold men. And wherever in our history a death-defying band of warriors has joined together to fight off terrible enemies, to awaken the people, and to kindle new fire in their hearts, they have felt akin to this wild, daring hunt:[130]

---

[129] See footnote 89 in the previous chapter "The Holy Bread."
[130] From the song "Lützows wilde Jagd" ("Lützow's Wild Hunt") written by the soldier Theodor Körner in 1813 during the German war of liberation against the French under Napoleon.

It comes down this way in dark rows,
And blaring horns sound in it,
And fill the soul with terror

In the German Alps, such crowds still hold their processions during the Twelve Nights. Where they stomp across the dead fields, the farmer knows that these will bear double the fruit in the coming year. For Wotan, whom they hear riding along on a snorting white horse, is at the same time the benevolent giver of growth and harvest.

But the storm is followed by a great calm. The light that was born in the night of the year has proven its strength in the storm, and its quiet growth overcomes the power of the unchanging world from within. The folk custom, the faithful mirror of our yearly life, also reveals an eternal truth. Three kings wander through the land with star and crown; they knock on doors and ask for gifts, and wherever they enter a field or walk through a grove, earth and tree reward them with double gifts. They are said to be the wise men from the East, of whom the Bible tells us, but we call them kings, and whereas there they bring gifts of reverence to the new Lord, here they bring new life itself. They carry the star with them, but for us this is the ancient sign of the year. In many places it is even a wheel, which is set in motion by the three kings— as a sign that the wheel of the year has now begun to turn again, and with it the earthly cycles, and that all must stand still on the twelfth night, if they did not wish to arouse the wrath of the white horse rider[131] and Frau Holle.[132]

---

[131] Referring to Odin, who in the Norse tradition rides the eight-legged horse Sleipnir.

[132] Frau Holle, known in some regions as Holda or Hulda, is a figure in Germanic mythology. She is said to live at the bottom of a well, reminiscent of the Norns, and to look after the spirits of children who die as infants. She was celebrated during the twelve days of Yule,

Our own written sources, however, which bear witness to sacred primordial times, tell us of the three gods who created human life and destiny out of trees by the roaring sea:

Then from the throng / did three come forth,
From the home of the gods, / the mighty and gracious;
Two without fate / on the land they found,
Ask and Embla, / empty of might.

Soul they had not, / sense they had not,
Heat nor motion, / nor goodly hue;
Soul gave Odin, / sense gave Hönir,
Heat gave Lothur / and goodly hue.[133]

Even older northern myths, recorded in faraway India, tell of the three divine brothers who go with the year, and who begin the course of their year on the holy nights. At the other end of the world, among the cliffs of Scandinavia, these three can still be seen carved in stone: they hold the wheel of the year, just as our three kings carry the wheel star of the year. In the north the three are called High, Just-as-High, and Third;[134] in India they are called the Walking, the Shining and

a transition period between calendar years, hence Plassmann's reference to the cycle of the year standing still. During the Christian era, she became associated with witchcraft, and even carried a distaff, a tool used in weaving that resembles the broomstick now associated with witches in popular culture. Her name is cognate with the Modern German adjective *hold* (lovely, fair, favorable). She is likely a northern equivalent to Perchta/Berchta. She is also likely related the *Hulder/Huldra*, a forest nymph in Scandinavian folklore.

[133] Stanzas 12-18 of *Völuspá*, a poem of the Edda. Translation by Henry Adams Bellows.

[134] These are names under which Odin appears to King Geirrod in *Gylfaginning* (*The Beguiling of Gylfi*), a story in the Prose Edda compiled by Snorri Sturluson. This source is considered less reliable for accurate and authentic information about old Norse religion and

the Third in the Waters. These three divine brothers have also been faithfully preserved in our fairy tale. They are the three brothers sent by their father to fetch the water of life. All three endure many adventures and dangers, but only the third reaches the goal and finds the water of life. They all three lead up the coming year, but only the third leads it to the end; for they are the coming, the turning, and the receding year.

For many thousands of years these three wanderers have made their yearly journey, bringing light and life, since they first awakened the higher life of humanity at the edge of the northern sea. They will continue to walk through the millennia if we faithfully preserve with them the heritage of the ancestors.

---

mythology than the original poetic sources. These names have nothing to do with three brothers, or with the year.

22

Die Mütternacht

MOTHERS' NIGHT

Wherever Germanic people live and have taken root on this vast earth, the Christmas tree lights up around the winter solstice. The wintergreen tree, which blossoms in lights in the middle of the night, has become a symbol of Germans, and the archetype of our experience of the world. In the east and southeast of the Reich, the ring of settlements stretches far and wide that Germans who plough the land have created among the confusion of foreign peoples and tribes; but everywhere, in the Bohemian Forest, in the Spiš,[135] in the scattered settlements of the Carpathians[136] and far overseas, the lights on the tree that has become the tree of the Germans blaze on Christmas Eve. Wherever a people expands its living space, it takes its household gods with it in order to remain true to itself; be it earth from the sacred homeland soil, high-seated pillars from the hall, or

---

[135] A region of present-day Slovakia once settled by German farmers, called *Zips* in German.

[136] A mountain range that arcs across Central and Eastern Europe.

consecrated customs in which the people's experience of the world is contained. What is the tree of light for us today has many predecessors, and this symbol of the world tree has absorbed many similar traditions. The topping tree[137] is an example, which bold Vikings took with them from their Nordic homeland to Iceland and across the ocean to faraway Vinland.[138] And the blue light on the tree, which we light today for all our brothers on earth, near and far, is deeply related to the light that was once burned for the love of those who were far away on a dangerous sea voyage, or who were looking for new land on which to start new lights of the people's life.

For as it is today, so it was in ancient times. Everything we learn from ancient writers about the customs and beliefs of our ancestors touches us like glad tidings from primordial times, because we feel the deep kinship across millennia that is a guarantee for the permanence in our soul and being. Germanic peoples had wandered far and had fought for new homes beyond the borders of the Roman Empire with sword and plough; but even here they faithfully preserved what had once grown in their homeland. The Angles had emigrated from their Holstein homeland,[139] settled in Britain and finally become Christians. But still around the year AD 700, the

---

[137] An ancient Germanic building custom still practiced today in Scandinavia, German-speaking countries, the Netherlands, and many English-speaking countries, including North America, in which a tree is placed on the roof of a newly constructed building after the last beam is placed, originally done to appease the tree spirits displaced during construction.

[138] The Norse name for North America.

[139] The Angles were one of several Germanic tribes from what is now northern Germany, the Netherlands, and Denmark that settled in England, the others being predominantly Saxons, Jutes, and Frisians. Holstein is a region of northern Germany and was indeed the original homeland of the Angles.

Christian priest Bede[140] wrote of their Christmas customs:

> They began the year when we celebrate the birth of the Lord. That very night, which we hold so sacred, they used to call by the heathen word *Modraniht*, that is, "mothers' night," because of the ceremonies they performed all that night.[141]

Does this name "Night of the Mothers" or "Mothers' Night" from the young days of our people not touch us like a very familiar memory of our own childhood? It is the night consecrated to the mystery of motherhood, in prescient relation to that great experience of the rebirth of the sun from the abyss of the world, the mother's womb of all being. The mother with child today forms to a large extent the emotional content of the festival, for this emotional content is also an ancient inheritance, for the human couple with the child under the world tree is an idea that is certainly very closely connected with the consecration customs of the Mother's Night. But the name contains even more. We know from many monuments, and in our folk customs and fairy tales it still resonates today, which among the most familiar figures of our native faith are the three mothers who, as bearers of womanly wisdom and motherly kindness, go through the land at this time, distributing gifts and giving people good advice and good thoughts, especially those who have a child in the cradle.

This idea was so deeply rooted in our people two thousand years ago that even Germanic Roman officials who ruled

---

[140] Bede was an English monk who, around AD 731, wrote his historically invaluable *Ecclesiastical History of the English People*. At this time, the conversion of the Anglo-Saxon peoples to Christianity was mostly complete.

[141] From Bede's *De Temporum Rationae* (*The Reckoning of Time*).

along the German Rhine had consecration stones set to these three mothers who guard the newborn. When the Romans gave way, and new Germanic tribes came, even they knew of the three mothers a thousand years later. And the housewives used to lay the table for them on holy nights, with food and drink and lay three knives so that the three sisters, as they were called, could feast. Pious zealots may have railed against this, but the motherly sisters reside too firmly in the hearts of the people, and so they, who are known by the names Einbede, Warbede and Willibede, [142] have even had a monument erected to them in Worms Cathedral.

But the Germanic legend and fairytale have preserved them even more firmly with all their features. The holy nights, in which the new light and the new year are born, belong to them; that is why they appear everywhere at the cradle of the newborn and give him their gifts. In Bavaria they are called the "*Heilrätinnen*," or more often the "*Perchten*," [143] which means the shining ones, because they accompany the light at its birth. They are invited as guests by the people and prove to be friendly and helpful to the good. We know them— admittedly in quadruplicate rather than a trio—from the fairy tale of Sleeping Beauty, to whom they bestow the good gifts of life that finally triumph over the evil influence of the thirteen. In the old Norse tale of the Norn Guest, [144] the good sisters kindle the child's light of life; here, the inner connection with our Christmas festival of light becomes particularly clear. And since they have been appearing as a

---

[142] These are the names of the three *Beten*, Catholic saints in the southern part of the German-speaking world. Plassmann's assumption that these stem from the same Germanic *Matronaes* (three female deities) he discusses in this passage is controversial.

[143] See the previous chapter "On the Wild Host and the Three Wanderers" for a discussion of Perchta.

[144] *Nornagests þáttr*, a Norse heroic saga written around 1300.

holy trinity since time immemorial, bringing their gifts to the child, and are full of wisdom, they may well have communicated much of their nature to the wise men from the East, of whom neither number nor name is known, and may even be the actual original figures of the numerous Epiphany plays.[145]

Ancient myths and eternally relevant legends tell of the three mothers who sit at the foot of the world tree and spin the threads of all becoming.[146] The night is consecrated to them, which we celebrate as consecration nights, just as our ancestors did. To descend to these mothers, as a great poet put it, means to stop at the living roots of our being, which today has found a symbol that spans the entire earth in the shining world-tree.

---

[145] This is a particularly far-fetched idea of Plassmann's.
[146] In the Norse tradition these are the Norns. A connection between Mothers' Night and the Norns is very plausible, as well as to the Dísir, mysterious female deities worshipped during the Dísablót (Sacrifice to the Dísir) in Scandinavia around the same time of year. These traditions may have once been analogous regional variations of a similar religious festival.

23

Die Goldenen Äpfel

THE GOLDEN APPLES

The deep knowledge of what our people wrote about themselves, how they interpreted their lives and their meaning, is still contained in our fairytales. We hear of the bold king's son who fears nothing; of the poor youth who carries within himself the high calling to become the king of the golden mountain; of the soldier who makes a pact with death and the devil, only to ultimately emerge victorious over both because he fearlessly and boldly goes his own way. It is always the chosen hero who, through hardship and danger, makes his way to the place where the water of life flows, which gives immortality, and where the grove stands, in the middle of which grows the tree with the golden apples—the apples of life, to eat from which means eternal life. But even more than that, to eat them will reveal the meaning of life, which in itself means eternity and immortality.

And yet the grove with the golden apples does not lie in some inaccessible realm that no living person can reach. It is true that everywhere along the way there are hardships and dangers, enemies and adventures, but what leads us over all these obstacles is a pure mind and a courageous heart. The land of golden apples lies within us—it is the land in the deep well into which Gold-Maria descends to rise again as a golden maiden. For she has shaken the tree with the fruit, she has baked the bread and milked the cows, and since she has done all this in the right spirit, for the common good and for the sake of the cause itself, she finds the right way, and she returns rich and honored from the inner land. But Pech-Maria, who in all this thought only of herself, who let fruit, bread, and milk go to waste, she returns with shame from the land where man's true worth is weighed and his inner nature becomes visible.[147]

This orchard where the tree with the golden apples stands is the field of activity and self-assertion that is decided in the cycle of the year, where work and harvest, activity and gain follow one another eternally. In the center of this grove of the year stands the tree with the golden apples, on which the golden-feathered bird sits, and whose golden apples form the circle of the year, as drawn by the sun on the horizon. The tree stands where the sacred center of the year is; at the bottom of the well into which the sun descends to rise again, rejuvenated and with new vitality, with all who follow its eternal laws. There they will find the new light and the golden fruits, which can only be broken by those who have the proper courage and the right attitude, who are able to bear silently the hardships that evil powers and spirits do to them. It is the tree of the midwinter season, of the holy nights when the sun and people turn inwards to contemplate themselves.

In primordial times, our ancestors experienced this depth of the year far more powerfully, for they were more directly confronted with life and its dangers than we, who sit as if in

---

[147] A reference to the fairy tale of Goldmarie and Pechmarie. Pech (n.) means misfortune.

a well-filled larder and have lost the sense of life itself, along with the sense of its dangers. The fruit of the year lay piled up in the barns and larders, the only guarantee of life through a long winter and a distant spring. So the golden fruit of the apple tree might well become a symbol of the golden sun itself under which it had ripened, the nuts seeming to contain the life of the sun itself. This is the essence of the fairytale, in which the nuts on the tree of life contain a dress as radiant as the sun. So the custom of building a frame on which eight golden apples hang at Christmas must also go back to ancient times; for this frame is an image of the course of the year itself, and the lights correspond to the golden apples. Nor is the bird that sits on the world-tree missing. This is also the meaning of the gilded nuts that still hang on our Christmas tree today; the nuts that in the fairytales of Cinderella and Thousandfurs[148] turn the poor girl into a royal bride in a golden robe. The hero who wins the golden apples from the distant orchard in our fairy tale is none other than that ancient sun-hero who, as Heracles in Greek myth, fetches the apples from the sacred grove guarded by the Hesperides, the daughters of the night. To the people he is the archetype of the brave German man who goes his way regardless of danger and hardship, thanks or ingratitude, because he recognizes the meaning of his own life in regaining the fruits for the whole people.

---

[148] A fairy tale titled *Allerleirauh* in German, in which a king promises his dying wife that he will not remarry unless it is to a woman as beautiful as her. The only woman in the kingdom as beautiful as his late wife is his own daughter, and so the king sets his eyes on her. In some versions of the tale, the girl is cracking nuts one day when, inside one of the nuts, she finds a beautiful dress as golden as the sun, which enables her to attend a ball in another kingdom and attract the attention of the prince there, whom she marries instead of her father.

The image of this sacred tree with its golden fruit is widespread among many peoples, but only the people of the original northern homeland and their relatives in other countries[149] have preserved its true meaning. Our people have faithfully held on to their ancient knowledge in myths and customs against foreign falsification. For us, as thousands of years ago, the tree with the golden apples is the image of true knowledge: the knowledge of pure life and its eternal laws.

For a time, a strange magic has been able to fill this sacred cycle of the year with dark spooky figures and to turn it into a magic circle of inhospitable powers. But anyone who seriously digs for the treasures that rest in the sacred native soil will encounter the same fate as the treasure seeker of whom our greatest poet sang. Out of the black, stormy night, the boy with the shining bowl comes to meet him, and like a reminder from the joyful past, he hears his words:

Taste the draught of pure existence
Sparkling in this golden urn,
And no more with baleful magic
Shalt thou hitherward return.
Do not seek for treasures longer;
Let thy future spell-words be,
Days of labor, nights of resting:
So shall peace return to thee![150]

---

[149] Referring to Indo-European peoples.
[150] The final stanza of the poem *The Treasure-Seeker* (*Der Schatz-gräber*) by Johann Wolfgang von Goethe.